Josiah H. Temple

History of the First Sabbath School in Framingham, Mass., from 1816 to 1868

With a sketch of the rise of Sabbath schools

Josiah H. Temple

History of the First Sabbath School in Framingham, Mass., from 1816 to 1868
With a sketch of the rise of Sabbath schools

ISBN/EAN: 9783337097561

Printed in Europe, USA, Canada, Australia, Japan

Cover: Foto ©ninafisch / pixelio.de

More available books at **www.hansebooks.com**

HISTORY

OF THE

FIRST SABBATH SCHOOL

IN

FRAMINGHAM, MASS.,

FROM 1816 TO 1868;

WITH A

SKETCH OF THE RISE OF SABBATH SCHOOLS.

By J. H. TEMPLE.

"The historian must first of all give an accurate record of facts in their just order; but if the Past is to speak persuasively to the Present, it must be so reanimated as to bring to view living men and scenes, that the imagination may be enlisted and the pulse quickened."

BOSTON:
PRINTED FOR THE AUTHOR BY WRIGHT & POTTER,
No. 4 SPRING LANE.
1868.

PREFATORY NOTE.

An attempt has been made to gather up, from the scanty records existing, and from the memories of its early founders, the history of a Sabbath school: to trace the working of causes, and note their incidental and full results.

That the effort to collect these scattered materials was made none too soon, is apparent from the fact that no public record is extant, and *only one person now living** has been found who can give the date of the formation of the school.

Though the design is necessarily limited, and the facts set forth have a strictly local value, yet, as tracing the development of a common purpose, and as a picture of the times when the Sabbath school had its rise, perhaps this little book may possess an interest beyond our own community.

The idea of gathering classes of children on the Sabbath for catechetical and Biblical instruction, was not a new one, a half century ago. Individuals, moved by their own impulses, and by Christian principle, had collected a few children at their houses, or some convenient room, and taught them the Scrip-

---

* Mrs. Matthew Gibbs.

tures, and sought to lead them in the ways of piety. Societies had, to some extent in this country, and very generally in Great Britain, been formed to teach *the children of the poor* the elements of reading and religion on Sunday, because that was their only day of leisure.

But the thought of collecting children into schools on the Sabbath solely for religious instruction, and of making these schools co-operative with public worship in the promotion of Scriptural knowledge and godliness, had not taken intelligent and definite shape in this country before 1814 or 1815.

Thus the school in Framingham was one of the earliest parish schools established. And the history of its formation and growth will be substantially the history of the formation and growth of all our New England Sabbath schools.

INTRODUCTORY.

1814.

The first steps towards gathering a class of youth for religious instruction, in Framingham, were taken by Miss Nancy Bent and Miss Abagail Stone.

These young ladies, who were intimate friends, mutually agreed to make an effort, each in her own circle of acquaintances, to establish a weekly meeting of children of both sexes, for the special purpose of moral and religious improvement. The leading object was the study of the Bible. This was in the summer of 1814.

Miss Stone formed a class of those living in what is now the village of Saxonville, which met on Saturday afternoons at the house of her grandfather, Colonel Micah Stone.* How many children joined the class, and from what families, cannot be ascertained.

---

* The house stood on the corner, near the large elms, opposite the counting-room of the Corporation.

At the same time Miss Bent invited the children of her neighbors to meet her at her father's house,—also on Saturday afternoons. The children of the Boynton, Abbott, Hastings, and Herring families, and some others, to the number of fourteen or fifteen, accepted the invitation.

These children were from four to ten years old. They would start from home soon after dinner, taking their *braiding*,—which was the child's work of those days, and at which they could keep busy without interfering with their recitations. They were received at the old mansion—so shaded by spreading oaks and fragrant locust trees—with a cordial welcome, which made the most timid feel quite at home.

Some had learned lessons from the Catechism, others had committed single stanzas or entire hymns from Watts' "Divine Songs," and others verses of Scripture, which they in turn recited, and received kind words of commendation, and suggestion, and encouragement, as the case required.

When the prepared lessons had been heard, the teacher would tell them a story from the Bible, or speak to them of personal religious duty, and close the exercises with prayer.

These classes continued to meet, respectively at Deacon Bent's and Colonel Stone's, through the warm weather for two seasons; and this effort of these young ladies may properly be regarded as the pioneer, if not the germ of the Sabbath school.

1816.

The two years previous to 1816 were remarkable for the special religious interest which prevailed throughout the town. Between September, 1815, and September, 1816, fifty-three were admitted into the Baptist church, and between the summer of 1814 and the fall of 1816, sixty-nine joined the Congregational church. The newly received members—especially those in youth—were not forward to take a prominent part in public duties; but such as had made profession in previous years, and received a new quickening from this gracious visit of the Spirit, were ready to meet the new calls of duty.

In the summer of 1816 Miss Abagail Bent spent some weeks in Bath, N. H., where a Sabbath school was already in existence, and where she had become warmly enlisted in the good work. On her return, late in August, she perhaps suggested, certainly entered heartily into a movement for starting a Sabbath school in connection with the Congregational church.

This method of Christian labor was comparatively new in this country. The Sunday schools of England were peculiar to her institutions, and were not a pattern for us. Only isolated schools had been organized in this State, and these mainly as individual enterprises, or charity schools. Probably not more than nine parish schools had been instituted before the summer of 1816,—ours being the *tenth* in the order of time. But the plan held out sure promise of rich and good results, and was readily taken hold of by those of congenial spirit.

On Sabbath, the first day in September, (1816,) a consultation was held, at which were present Miss Abagail Bent, Miss Mary Brown, (Mrs. Jonas Colburn,) Miss Martha Trowbridge, (Mrs. Matthew Gibbs,) Miss Mary Haven, Mrs. Uriah Rice, and Mrs. Charles Fiske; when it was decided to collect a class of girls, as a beginning of a Sabbath school.

Only ladies were present at this first consultation. There was no public sentiment in Framingham in favor of the enterprise. Only a few could be relied on to help it forward, as only a few, who had a heart for it, were sufficiently well educated and experienced in teaching to take so public a position. But in the consciousness of a good cause, these few quietly set to work. No public notice was given. Each invited her own particular friends; and on the next Sabbath—September 8th—at the intermission of public worship, a considerable number of girls was gathered in the Academy Hall, (the brick building which was taken down in 1837,) where they recited such lessons from the Assembly's Shorter Catechism as they had prepared, (most children were then taught the Catechism at home very early in life, and could recite it at pleasure,) or repeated hymns, or Scripture verses. No separate classes were formed at this time, and no lessons were assigned; but each studied what was suited to her age, or taste, or her parents' wishes. Miss Brown, Miss Trowbridge, and Miss Haven were uniformly present, and took part in instructing the children. Mrs. Fiske and two or three other ladies was generally in attendance to render aid, and give a moral support to the enterprise.

Usually some male member of the church would come in and open the exercises with prayer, but in the absence of these, Miss Brown would perform the duty.

They continued to meet every Sabbath till the coming on of winter. There was no fire in the hall, and the little children found difficulty in keeping warm. One of them says: "I well recollect one very cold day, when I sat shivering while one of the teachers went in search of some man to open the school with prayer. The minutes were very long till Dr. Cotton came."

The Sabbath after the consultation already mentioned, Miss Abagail Bent proposed to one of the ladies interested, that they should collect a class of boys in the old Town House. But the proposal was declined, on the ground that it was properly the duty of the male professors to teach the lads.

Whether the suggestion was made to them by Miss Bent is not known, but the men were found ready to undertake their part of the work. Abner Stone, Luther Haven, and Samuel Murdock agreed to take charge of a class of boys.

Notice was given from the pulpit, and on the next Sabbath—the third in September—those boys who had in part formed the class that met the two previous seasons at Deacon Bent's, and a few others, collected at the Town House, and a school was opened.

They continued to meet till about November 1st. Mr. Stone and Mr. Murdock heard the older boys recite, and Miss Bent took charge of the small ones. Miss Bent called her class into the floor for recitation, after the manner of common schools, the others remained in their seats.

These children, like those in the Academy Hall, prepared lessons in the Assembly's Catechism, or learned hymns and portions of Scripture.

Thus began our Sabbath school.

With so many discomforts and inconveniences, and so little that was attractive in their surroundings, did these teachers and pupils enter upon their new work. From so small beginnings arose the system which has been the source of invaluable blessings to so many of us.

Neither place was intended for or adapted to such a purpose. The Academy Hall occupied nearly the whole upper story of the building and was unfurnished, except with fixed seats—without desks—at the sides, and movable benches without backs, to be used as occasion required.

The old Town House—built from materials of the meeting-house taken down in 1808—was still larger. The room—embracing the entire edifice—was most forbidding and uncomfortable. The only inside finish was a ceiling of boards up to the windows, and plastering without painting. The whole interior was blackened by age; the corners and window-caps were covered with spiders' webs; and the flies and wasps had possession of the rattling windows, when it was sufficiently warm. There was neither fireplace nor stove. The seats—running lengthwise of the building—were made of oaken planks, very narrow, with hard pine backs; each range rising one step up an inclined plane from the floor to the sides, and were so high that the smaller children could not touch the floor with their feet. There was a platform across the east end of the floor, with a fixed table in front, suitable for holding books and papers.

The house, as its name implies, was owned by the town, and was used by the inhabitants for town meetings, and for military and political purposes; and consequently had none of the sacred character and associations which attach to a church or vestry, or even a schoolhouse.

The more prominent and influential boys did not join the school, and looked with some contempt on those whose parents required them to attend. They would gather about the door to tease those who went in, and sometimes would disturb the quiet of the school by throwing chips into the open door,—so little did they reverence the old house, and so little did they care for religious things.

With our comfortable room, and convenient arrangements, and sacred associations, we may well look back with wonder to those days when our fathers and mothers first went to the Sabbath school. And not unlikely some of us are ready to conclude that we would not risk the cold feet, and hard seats, and taunts of our mates.

But our fathers and mothers—however they might have felt at the time—do not now think of their discomforts; they are glad that they took all the risks and suffered all the inconveniences. They learned the precious truths of God's holy Word, and those lessons and hymns which now they prize so much,—which they love to recall, and whose "meditation" is so sweet. That was the gate by which they entered "wisdom's ways," which are "pleasantness," and her paths which are "peace."

And we may well dwell with grateful admiration on this small beginning,—this grain of mustard-seed planted in the earth. Probably not more than forty in all attended both departments this first season. But the teachers were not discouraged. They started in faith, and persevered in hope.

The Sabbath school was a new thing. The schools in Beverly and Concord—the first to be formed in the State—were started only six years before. And while the motive was well defined and worthy, and the end desirable, the idea was yet in a crude state; the mode of gaining the ends desired unsettled; the relation of the Sabbath school to the church not at all comprehended. No well-arranged system of conducting Sabbath schools had been devised. They were patterned somewhat after the common schools, which then were managed on no accepted system,—each teacher adopting his own method of instruction.

And the popular sentiment had not become enlisted in favor of Sabbath school instruction. It was really against it. The leading families stood aloof and looked with distrust on the movement, and did not allow their children to attend. Many good men were in doubt about the wisdom of the experiment. The best men, in some instances, felt that it was to become eventually a substitute for family religious instruction, which had been a leading feature of our New England society from the first, and which was undoubtedly a prime element in keeping alive the Puritan spirit and faith. And added to this was the wide-spread conviction among conscientious Christians, that the labor of teaching a Sabbath school was contrary to the spirit if not the letter of the fourth Commandment. This conviction grew partly out of *the sacred regard for holy time* then prevalent, and partly from the notion of the Sabbath school derived from the schools in England established by Robert Raikes, which were half secular in their design,—the elements of *reading* being taught as well as the elements of religion.

It required some self-denial to enlist in the work in these circumstances. We must give credit for some moral courage and some disinterested motives. We can readily believe that a true Christian zeal, a desire to honor the Saviour, actuated these teachers. We can readily believe that it was God's good Spirit which prompted the effort, and which gave it success.

The results were immediate, and were decided enough to satisfy the most sanguine, and of a character to fill the pious heart with joy. Most of these teachers lived to see the assured success of their plans, and to reap the first fruits of their labors. They rejoiced in what they were able to do to nurture the children of that generation in "the fear of the Lord." They had the satisfaction of welcoming many of these lambs into the Saviour's fold,—of sitting with them in heavenly places in Christ Jesus.

And many of these—teachers and pupils—we fully believe are now sitting in the heavenly places on Mount Zion above,—are now studying the great truths of God, brought first to their notice in His revealed Word, which they commenced to study in the Sabbath school; are now tracing out the wondrous plan of Redemption through a crucified Saviour, in whom they believed and through whom they were saved; are now receiving an hundred-fold for the labors and sacrifices of their brief Christian life.

1817.

In the spring of 1817, public notice was given from the pulpit, and about the middle of May the children of both sexes were gathered in the Town House, and a regular school was opened. The room had lost none of its forlorn appearance, and gained no additional comforts. The children clustered themselves in groups according to previous acquaintance, the boys taking the north and the girls the south side of the room. In due time they were divided into classes, partly according to age, and partly to accommodate the number of teachers in attendance.

Deacon Luther Haven was by general request induced to act as Superintendent.

The teachers, in addition to those who took hold the last fall, were Anna Haven, (Mrs. H. G. Foster,) Nancy Gibbs, (Mrs. Aaron Bailey,) Betsey Gibbs, (Mrs. Martin Rice,) Jane Walker, (Mrs. Ebenezer Stone,) Abagail Stone, (Mrs. Samuel Murdock,) and Mrs. Charles Fiske.

There were in all eight or nine classes,—a very pleasing advance on the state of things at the first opening of the school in the previous September. As some of the teachers were absent during July and August, engaged as teachers in the public schools, the whole number on the list necessarily more than equals the number of classes. And the deficiency of male teachers made it necessary that several classes of lads should be taught by females.

The younger classes studied Emerson's Catechism, which was now introduced, and was continued in use for not less than fifteen years. The older classes studied Scripture lessons, the Assembly's Catechism, or Cummings' Questions on the historical parts of the New Testament.

A rule—perhaps not expressly stated, but certainly acted upon—which had an important influence in shaping the Sabbath school at this early stage was, that only those of sufficient education and age to qualify them to teach in district schools, ought to be expected to become teachers. This accounts for the absence of some who would otherwise have taken an active part in the school; and it accounts for the systematic and orderly arrangement which obtained from the outset. After a few years, from the increase of classes and other causes, this rule was somewhat relaxed.

In many towns, when a Sabbath school was first established, it was conducted without much regard to order, and without a responsible head. Each teacher—and sometimes each scholar—was a law unto himself. When a class had finished the lesson it was dismissed and retired, thus causing more or less confusion. In some instances, it is known that each scholar was allowed to leave as soon as he had said his verse or lesson, and not always in the quietest manner; and it would thus happen that the attraction outside would quickly become stronger than that in the class. No interested attention was secured to instruction, and at best the work was a set task which was hurried through as rapidly as possible, and probably left no very serious or pleasant impressions on the mind. This, however, happened a year or two later, after Sabbath schools became more common, and were opened because the tide of public sentiment set that way.

But no such irregularity or want of system characterized our school. There was general decorum observed in assembling, the exercises were opened with prayer, the school was continued about an hour, and was dismissed in form.

The high personal character of the teachers engaged, and the Christian motives which actuated them, gave a tone and impulse to the school, as well as imposed a healthful moral restraint, and made it in all respects an appropriate part of Sabbath labor. It was from the outset, consecrated solely to moral and religious instruction.

Dr. Kellogg from the first took a true interest in the prosperity of the school, and gave it his sanction and hearty support, and the benefit of his judicious counsel; though it was not, in those days, regarded as a part of ministerial duty to engage personally in Sabbath school instruction.

In this second year most of the decidedly religious families gave their influence in favor of the school, and sent their *young children.*

It was a peculiar feature of the earliest movement, that all concerned should regard it as intended for young children. Those of fourteen and upwards felt that they were *too old* to become pupils, and thus parts of families would be in the school, and parts would stand aloof,—often to the discouragement of those who were almost too old to go, and yet not quite exempt. Few—of the boys especially—remained in their classes after they reached fifteen. And this feeling had its influence for several years,—perhaps till the youngest of the earliest classes had grown up. So hard is it to supplant opinions once adopted; so vitally important is it that early impressions be right; so deeply do first habits take root in the heart.

In this and the few following years there was no library for the use of the pupils. Says one of the then teachers: "We had no library. A collection would be taken once a year to purchase books to be given as presents to the scholars, each teacher selecting the books for his or her class." Many of these little books received as presents, are now in existence in the families then connected with the school. They are of a strictly evangelical character, and though some of them were too abstract for the ready comprehension of young children, yet their influence on the taste, and aspirations, and moral conclusions could not but be of a healthy and elevating nature,—in striking contrast with the children's literature of the present day!

The few books then in reach of families, was a feature of the times which had its advantages as well as its evils. The few were better read; the contents came before a mind less occupied with facts and less filled with images; the truths set forth, by their singleness and distinctness, arrested attention and became incorporated in the moral life, and guided thought and belief. And without a library to divide the interest and time, the simple hymns committed, or the Scripture verses, or the comprehensive answers in the Catechism, made a permanent impression. The truths received remained in contact with the mind till the next Sabbath school lesson was learned. And a library book—especially if a fascinating story—would only have confused or partially effaced the impression of that lesson. Both the textbook and the library book being a part of the Sabbath school, would have an equal value and equal sacredness in the view of the unreasoning child. Hence perhaps the library book may in part nullify the effect of the lesson.

At any rate, the lessons recited in the Sabbath school in 1816, 1817 and 1818, became fixed in the memory. The then children of five, now the men and women of fifty-five, can repeat the texts and hymns with readiness and accuracy, while their efforts to recall the lessons learned in the common schools at the same period are almost complete failures. So in harmony with the deep cravings of the soul in its earlier and purer life, are the simple and vital revelations of God's Word! So exactly adapted is this Holy Word to the child and the man! So divine and benevolent was the purpose of Him who gave this revelation as a "light to the feet" and a "lamp to the path" which leads to "life eternal."

As appears from the facts now gathered, the original intention of our Sabbath school was *religious instruction*. It was, primarily, to store the minds of children with the facts and doctrines of the Bible. Watts' "Divine Songs," from which mothers and teachers selected the hymns to be taught their little ones, were strictly Scriptural in thought and language. Emerson's Catechism, in both the doctrinal and historical parts, was purely Scriptural. Direct answers to almost every question might have been given by quoting the inspired record, and the reason for giving the answer in his own language, appears to be for the sake of brevity and convenience in studying the lesson. The Assembly's Shorter Catechism, though broad in its general design, was drawn directly from the Bible, and was fortified at every step by Scripture quotations. Wilbur's Biblical Catechism was composed of a series of questions, to be answered by reciting *verbatim*, texts of Scripture.

Such was the purpose and method of those who founded the Sabbath school. To pass an idle hour was not in their thought. To amuse the children, and make the school attractive to their fancy and taste was not in the plan. The principle of emulation, even, was little appealed to. The auxiliary aid of music was not brought in. The *winning power of Christian love*, and *the inherent value of the truths learned* were mainly relied on, to awaken and keep up interest. They sought rather to be able to say to their pupils, as Paul said to Timothy: "That from a child thou hast known the Holy Scriptures, which are able to make thee wise unto salvation, through faith which is in Christ Jesus."

1818.

Fortunately, the "Register of the Framingham Sabbath school" for 1818, is still preserved. This register was made out in a neat copy hand by Solomon Fay, who acted as Secretary till his sudden death in 1820.

As it will refresh the memory of some who were then pupils, and cannot fix the date of their entrance to the school, nor recall the names of their associates; and as it will possess permanent value to their friends and children as a memento of the dead and the living; and as it will furnish a life-picture of the school of that early day, the list of scholars is given entire.

Fanny Underwood, Emily Conant, Emeline Stone, Catherine Parker, Relief Butler, Eliza Hemenway, Mary F. Hemenway, Maria Stone, Nancy Hill, Mary Harrington, Rebeckah Butrick, Mary Gallot, Arethusa Underwood, Miranda Belknap, Louisa Edgell, Sally Belknap, Catherine Hemenway, Harriet Russell, Emeline Hemenway, Nancy Hemenway, Almira Hemenway, Lucy Winch, Mary Dadmun, Eliza Dadmun, Mary Moseman, Eliza Belknap, Abagail Rice, Catherine Belknap, Eunice Bent, Abagail Hunnewell, Eliza Ann Parker, Sephronia Walker, Mary Childs, Abagail Eames, Mary Herring, Martha Smith, Lucinda Winch, Susan Edmands, Martha Forrister, Frances Boyenton, Sally Flagg, Martha E. Stone, Wealthy Taylor, Emily Parker, Mary Boyenton, Helen C. Bell, Anna Putnam, Eliza Wenzell, Mary W. Brackett, Eliza Owen, Eleanor Belknap, Abby H. Forrister, Martha Hastings, Mary Bailey, Mary Abbott, Eliza C. Abbott, Mary Moulton, Louisa Moulton, Harriet Herring, Catherine Peterson, Eleanor Peterson, Sophia Rice, Lucy Thurston, Eliza Belcher, Nancy Howe, Maria Brown, Abagail Parmenter, Eleanor Goodenow, Lucy C. Bent, Clarissa Belknap, Eveline Belknap, Bathsheba Hemenway, Emily Larrabee, Grace Goddard, Eliza Brackett, Harriet Hemenway,

Elmira Jones, Emeline Bullard, Nelly Haven, Sally Winch, Elmira Stone, Emeline Hemenway, Sarah Stearns, Mary Ann Stearns, Mary Putnam, Sally Daniels, Olive Grant, Deborah Sawyer, Diantha Angier, Louisa Lovejoy, Elizabeth Haven, Olivia Butler, Harriet Hollowell, Abagail Dudley, Catherine Winch, Emeline Rugg, Jane Curtis, Lawson Davis, Thomas Hastings, Jr., Eliphalet Hastings, Charles Herring, Calvin Hemenway, Ephraim W. Edmands, Henry L. Stone, Hiram Cheney, Dana Stone, Hollis Hastings, George Haven, Eben Abbott, Perkins Boyenton, Cyrus Abbott, William Eames, William Brackett, William Dadmun, Jr., Josiah Abbott, Jr., Gardner Edmands, Richard W. Stearns, Aaron Hayden, Theodore L. Hastings, Phineas Stone, Elliot H. Wescot, John B. Dench, Stephen Hayden, Samuel Forrister, Luke Rugg, David E. Brackett, Abner Butrick, Archibald Bent, John Jones, Charles Flagg, David K. Brackett, Joseph Cutting, Horatio Stone, William Gallott, Almon Hemenway, William Hastings, 2d, Micah Newton, Asa Stone, Henry L. Buckminster, Edward Buckminster, Lothrop T. Richardson, Charles O. Goodenow.

The whole number is one hundred and forty-two,—ninety-seven girls and forty-five boys,—indicating a rapid growth, and a general interest on the part of parents. Deacon Luther Haven was chosen Superintendent. The teachers were Abner Stone, Samuel Murdock, Eben Eaton, Abagail Bent, Mary Brown, Martha Trowbridge, Mary Haven, Ann Haven, Nancy Gibbs, Betsey Gibbs, Jane Walker, Abagail Stone, and Mrs. Charles Fiske.

To show how the school was engaged this season, and to complete this picture, the Superintendent's report, which was published in the Boston Recorder, is subjoined :—

"*Framingham Sabbath School.*—The Sabbath school commenced for the season on the 20th of May, under the direction of a Superintendent and ten teachers, and closed the 20th of October, thus continuing in session twenty-three Sabbaths. During this time there were committed to memory and recited, answers in Doctrinal Catechism, 1,676 ; Historical Catechism, 1,646 ; Assembly's Shorter Catechism, 4,166 ; Wilbur's Catechism, 242 ; Baldwin's Catechism, 92 ; Cumming's Questions, 8,409 ; verses of Scripture, 5,984; stanzas of Hymns, 13,242,—amounting in all to 35,457. Whole number of scholars, 142 ; average number in attendance, 70. One girl, Nancy Hill, recited 1,048 verses of Scripture, 142 answers in Wilbur's Catechism, and 558 stanzas of Hymns. Another, Emily Conant, recited 2,018 answers in Cumming's Questions, 223 verses of Scripture, and 491 Hymns. Another, Fanny Underwood, recited 1,871 answers in Cumming's Questions, and 194 verses of Scripture. One girl, Helen C. Bell, recited 1,461 Hymns. Six little girls, Mary F. Hemenway, Arethusa Underwood, Nancy Hemenway, Almira Hemenway, Mary Bailey and Sally Belknap, recited 3,344 Hymns.

"One hour only on each Sabbath was appropriated to the instruction of the children. Their punctual attendance and good behavior merited the approbation of both teachers and parents, who earnestly pray, that the seed here sown may ere long spring up and bring forth fruit to the glory of God.

"O that Sabbath schools may soon be established throughout the Christian world! None will ever lament engaging in this pleasing employment; the satisfaction they may derive by instructing the youth in the first rudiments of Christianity will repay them fourfold."

Up to this time, and for several years, indeed

until 1823 or 1824, the school was kept only during the warmer months, opening in May and closing before the first of November. This was partly a matter of necessity, and partly a matter of custom. None of the earliest schools were kept through the winter. The children first gathered into them could not be comfortably provided for in the inclement weather. And a custom thus established acquires a sort of authority, which gives it force long after the occasion for it has ceased. With us, it was at first a matter of necessity to close in the autumn, as there was no means of heating the Town House. But in fact young children, and many adults did not go to church regularly in the winter, as there was no means of heating the meeting-house. It was not till 1823, that stoves were put up in Dr. Kellogg's church. The fathers and the boys kept warm as best they could; the mothers and the girls depended on extra clothing and on *foot-stoves*, in which live coals from the hearth were put before leaving home. Most families living within two miles went home at noon. Such as lived too far to go home and return, would hire a " noon-room " in the village, where they could eat lunch, and put fresh coals in their foot-stoves, and perhaps " hear and tell some new thing."

1819.

To judge of the true standing of our Sabbath school, we are not to bring it to the test of ideas and methods of the present day, but to try it by the standard of opinions then prevalent. It might be greatly defective if compared with the present school, and of superior excellence compared with the schools of those days.

That we may form a correct estimate of the school at the period under review, a brief extract is made from an address to the churches sent forth by the General Association of Massachusetts in 1818, embodying the views of the leading ministers in regard to Sabbath schools:

"The most successful methods of the religious instruction of children, we believe, are *Sabbath schools* and *Bible classes.* Such is the known and tried utility of these schools, that no town or district should be without one, where a pious and suitable teacher can be procured. The manner of conducting these schools is usually as follows: At each meeting the youth have portions of Scripture, or catechisms, or sacred hymns assigned them, to be committed and rehearsed at the next meeting. The children are divided into classes, a list of their names is taken, and an account kept of their good or bad performance. When they have recited well a certain number of times they are rewarded with a tract or small book, where it can be done with convenience. The teacher occasionally puts to each child some questions arising from the lesson, adapted to his age and improvement. The meetings are opened and closed with prayer, and, if practicable, the children are taught to sing a hymn at the close.

"Were this plan generally adopted, we are fully persuaded that it would be attended with the increasing smiles of Heaven upon the rising generation. What they acquire from the Divine Word, under the enlightening and renewing influences of the Holy Spirit, may be the beginning of that fund of wisdom and knowledge which are to be learned in the school of heaven, in the presence of God and the Lamb, and in the company of the spirits of the just made perfect."

The number of scholars in the Sabbath school this year was one hundred and nineteen, thirty-two of whom were not in attendance last year, showing a great change in the constituents of the school. The novelty was wearing off, which undoubtedly accounts for some absences; some began to consider themselves too old to go longer, and some left town.

Those who engaged as teachers for the first time, were Ebenezer Stone, Edmond M. Capen, Eliza Buckminster, (Mrs. Levi Eaton,) Nancy Bullard, (Mrs. Otis Fairbanks.)

Deacon Luther Haven was Superintendent.

Among the older girls a class was formed in Milner's Church History, as abridged by Miss Rebeckah Eaton. Miss Buckminster took charge of this class.

The new scholars this year were: Joanna Law, Isabella Bent, Caroline Manson, Phebe Manson, Sally Cobb, Eunice Edgell, Nancy Goodnow, Silvia Parmenter, Caroline Pratt, Lucy Green, Cornelia Maynard, Susan Bennett, Ann Goddard, Eliza Evers, Susan Cobb, Pliny Fay, Eli Fay, Trowbridge Forrister, Peter Brewer, Gilbert J. Childs, John A. Buttrick, Calvin W. Angier, Albert Dadmun, Joseph Phipps, Albert Dalrymple, Roswell P. Angier, John T. Kittridge, William Conant, Henry W. Hudson, Newell Butler, Henry R. Wheeler, Diah L. Eames.

The number of answers recited in the different catechisms was 6,743; Cumming's Questions, 2,829; Bible verses, 21,524; Hymns,

5,209; amounting in all to 36,305. As there was a loss in numbers of 17 per cent. the net gain over last year was 6,700 answers. The pupils taking the highest rank were Emily Conant, Fanny Underwood, Emeline Stone, Catherine Parker, Eliza Hemenway, Mary F. Hemenway, Maria Stone, Nancy Hill, Rebeckah Buttrick, Abagail Parmenter, George Haven, and Abner Buttrick.

1820.

Mr. Abner Stone, who helped form the school, and had been a teacher from the first, was chosen Superintendent. Additional teachers: Matthew Gibbs, Nancy Kellogg, Elmira Rice, (Mrs. Francis Bowers.) New scholars: Susan Hastings, Abagail Fairbanks, Margaret Thomson, Mary L. Temple, Angeline Eaton, Mary Ann Alden, Betsey R. Hyde, Angeline Forbes, Jerusia Parmenter, Clarissa Moulton, Lowly Ann Howe, Lydia Roach, Sarah Moore, Emily Hollowell, Martha ———, Eliza Hemenway, 2d, Peter Davis, Horatio Bartlett,—18. The whole number in attendance this year was 93,—66 girls and 27 boys. The number of answers recited in the various catechisms was 17,752; Cumming's Questions, 1,062; Hymns,

10,196; verses of Scripture, 12,025; making in all 41,035,—equal to a net gain from last year, after deducting the loss of scholars, of 10,000 answers. The scholars highest in rank in recitations were Maria Stone, Rebeckah Buttrick, Miranda Belknap, Abby H. Forrister, Mary L. Temple, Helen C. Bell, Mary W. Brackett, Eleanor Belknap, Diantha Angier, Betsey R. Hyde, Calvin W. Angier, Albert Dalrymple, Thomas Hastings, Jr., Ephraim W. Edmands, Henry L. Stone, Hollis Hastings, William Brackett.

A careful study of these statistics furnishes a clew to the leading elements of the school. It discloses the fact that the girls greatly excelled the boys in the number of Scripture verses recited, while the boys excelled the girls in recitations in the catechisms. The highest number of credit marks to any girl is 2,850,—to Nancy Hill, all for Bible verses; the highest number of credit marks to any boy is 877,—to William Brackett, 608 for answers in the Assembly's Catechism, 43 Bible verses, 226 Hymns.

The increase in the amount of study, and number of perfect lessons, is probably a true index of the growth and efficiency of the school. The number of pupils decreased in these three years 33 per cent.; while the number of lessons recited increased 15 per cent. The teachers and scholars were getting better acquainted; and where a class had a teacher whom they had learned to respect and love, that teacher's power to awaken interest and secure a large amount of faithful study increased from year to year. While the school was in any sense an experiment, there were causes of friction and depression on every hand, but when it became well established, the moral and social influences seemed to rally to its support, and directly to raise its standard and quicken its life.

1821--'22.

Mr. Abner Stone was Superintendent of the school for the years 1821 and '22.

So far as is known nothing of special interest in the regular working of the school occurred in these years.

Ezra Hemenway became connected with the school as a teacher. The number of pupils and the amount of work done cannot be ascertained; nor is the Superintendent's annual report preserved.

It was in this latter year, probably, that the *first library* for the use of the school was bought. A small sum of money was raised by personal solicitation from the leading church-members and others, and a selection made from the comparatively limited number of children's books then published. The library was composed of small books, mostly in paper covers, some of which might properly be called tracts. The following list is a sample: Shepherd of Salisbury Plain, Gooseberry Bush, Worlds Displayed, Pleasures of Piety in Youth, Little Henry and his Bearer, New Testament Stories, The Robber's Daughter, The Two Lambs, Alfred and Galba, Hymns for Infant Minds.

This small library of small books was yet a matter of great consequence to the school. It was a good collection for those days. The books were mostly new to the children, and they were of an interesting character. They were well written, and they were eagerly read. Some were essays on religious truth or personal duty, but to a considerable extent they were simple narratives of facts, or unadorned biographies. They were such pictures of life as carry internal evidence of reality, and this is always pleasing to the young. Distorted views, and extravagant notions, and highly colored sketches are not relished till the taste has become perverted. The child craves the simple truth.

The Dairyman's Daughter and the Shepherd of Salisbury Plain, so natural in incident, and direct in statement, and pure in style,—such homely pictures of homely life,—have been read with absorbing and tearful interest by tens of thousands in the seventy years since they were written; they are as eagerly read by children now, and they will continue to be read with the same concentrated interest by tens of thousands more, so long as the English language is preserved in its purity.

The size of these books was no test of their worth. Each of these small volumes contains as much of fact and variety of incident, and fresh thought, as the two hundred page religious novel, or the diluted, well spiced story, which now in our libraries take the places of these simple narratives of common life.

There is no record to show on what system the books were given out and returned.

In some cases, at this time, it was the custom to give them out once a month, to be kept for that length of time. In others, the books were lent out as a reward of special merit. When a pupil had been punctual in attendance, or faithful in study and perfect in recitations, at the end of a month, or once in two weeks, he or she was entitled to a book from the library;

and for superior excellence, two books were allowed to be taken out. Thus the library was made to serve the double purpose of a means of improvement, and an incentive to fidelity and careful study.

1823--'30.

Deacon Eben Eaton was chosen Superintendent in 1823, and continued in office till 1830. No records for these years have been preserved, but the school appears to have gone on peacefully and prosperously.

There is always a period between sowing and reaping, when there is a repetition of familiar processes, and a sameness of labor, and a patient waiting, which, though essential to vital growth and healthy development, has not the charm of novelty, and may be described in few words.

Such was this period in the history of our Sabbath school. And that it was filled up with watchful fidelity and patient, prayerful effort; that the classes were carefully instructed and the interests of the school conscientiously promoted, will appear in the results, when the time of the ingatherings of autumn comes.

Those may be more prominent and *seem* to deserve the highest honor, who plan and bring into successful action the elements of a great achievement, but without the after skill and endurance and persevering exertions, the beginning would fail, and the enterprise come to nought.

The new teachers in these years were Peter Parker, Alexander Abbott, Lambert Allen, Elbridge Bradbury, Asenath F. Eaton, Elizabeth Eaton, Eliza C. Abbott, Nancy Shepard, Emily S. Bell, Eliza Wenzell, Abby H. Forrister.

Those who joined the school as pupils at its first opening in 1816, now began to take charge of classes of little children.

During this period, *adult classes* began to become a feature of Sabbath schools. It was not in the original plan, but the system was adapted to such an addition. Indeed, it was not complete without it. No Sabbath school can present a more beautiful spectacle than that which embraces scholars of all ages, from lisping infancy to hoary-headed age,—" young men and maidens, old men and children."

The Sabbath School Union, in the report for 1827, mentions the fact that large numbers of young people were connecting themselves with the schools of their respective parishes. " Some, too, with locks blooming for the grave, said they would become Sabbath school scholars, and in accents tremulous with emotion gave thanks to God that they could now come and enjoy the privilege with which he was blessing their children." " In some towns," it is said, in the report for 1828, " almost the whole population from four to eighty-five years of age have become members of the Sabbath school."

In 1827 a class of young people of twenty and upwards, was formed in our Sabbath school. Moses Spofford, Electa Holden and others joined it. Peter Parker was perhaps its first teacher. This was probably the origin of the *Bible class* which continued to meet under different teachers, and with varied interest for many years. In 1829 it met during the warm season in the Town House, before the morning church service. In 1834 it met in the vestry of the H. E. Society, on Sabbath evenings. At first it was composed of both sexes; but afterwards, from increase of numbers, it was divided into two classes, one of males and one of females. Ultimately it became an integral part of the Sabbath school.

1829--'30.

We have now reached a period in the history of our Sabbath school when we naturally begin to look for the rounding up of primary results; when leading characteristics have acquired permanency; when tests may be applied to the past, and new and more enlarged plans be laid for the future.

Every year has its seasons. Every life has its stages,—more or less marked,—more or less distinctive,—each in some respects the sequence, in some the counterpart, of other stages,—but all intimately connected, and together forming one life. And every individual or associated plan or organization has stages of development and progress, when its active and passive agencies work and rest, when one influence or set of influences seem to be exhausted, and give place to something more vital. And each stage has its distinctive character, and may be studied by itself, and also as a component part of the whole.

Our school was such an organization. It had now reached its fourteenth year. The children of 1816 were no longer children, and the school was no longer an experiment. It had taken its place among the reliable religious agencies, and had made a history.

A general review of these fourteen years brings out some points of interest not specially dwelt upon in the preceding narrative. It was a well-defined era, having its own mission to accomplish. It comprised the period of *the gathering and organization* of Sabbath schools in this country. Nothing like a systematic and well-digested public effort on the part of the church for the promotion of Sabbath schools had been put forth previous to 1817. And the twelve succeeding years had been devoted mainly to the establishment, and increase of the number of schools and scholars, and to fix the true position of the Sabbath school as an auxiliary to public worship and pastoral labor. And so much success had attended these efforts that the Sabbath School Union was able to say in its report for 1829: " It is believed that a Sabbath school has been established in nearly every religious society in the State which is connected with the denominations united in the Union."

From this period onward the main effort of the State society, and all engaged in the work, was to elevate the character and enlarge the influence of Sabbath schools, and provide a suitable children's literature.

As regards our own school, looking back from this date, the change was great. Individual scholars were left, but none of the earliest classes remained. Younger brothers and sisters and new families had taken their places.

And of the first teachers, none remained. Deacon Haven and Abner Stone were still active members of the Sabbath School Society, and ready for any duty that would promote the prosperity of the school. One of the female teachers had died, and of the others some were married, and new duties demanded their time, and some had removed from town.

But of that devoted band who started the school, and carried it so successfully through its infancy, none turned against it, or ceased to love and cherish it. As a means of good, it fully met their expectations. And while kept from active participation in its duties by various causes, it ever had their full sympathy and their influence, and their counsels of matured experience.

A point of interest, as incidental to our development of the course of events, is the relation of the studies pursued in the Sabbath school to the general tone of religious sentiment in the church. A general rule must be, that the spirit of the one will correspond with the spirit of the other. The life of one will reflect itself in the life of the other. A prevalent formalism and accommodating spirit in the church, will lead to a course of instruction lacking the elements of vital godliness. The prevalence of pure evangelical doctrines will necessarily secure the adoption of text-books of an evangelical character.

This relation of cause and effect is well illustrated in our Sabbath school. The several seasons of religious interest enjoyed by the church during the eight years preceding the fall of 1816, had greatly raised the standard of Christian experience, and given unquestioned supremacy to evangelical thought and belief. The cross of Christ was "magnified" in the faith and practice of the church. Hence the prominence given in the Sabbath school to the study of the Scriptures. Hence the introduction of Emerson's Catechism, and the continued use of the Assembly's Shorter Catechism, so distinct in its enunciation of the leading doctrines of the Gospel. Hence it was only a natural result that when the church and Pastor, for Christ's sake, left the meeting-house of their fathers, at the division of the parish in 1829–30, the entire Sabbath school went with the church.

Although our school was one of the earliest of the public enterprises of the kind under-

taken, yet its foundation proved to be well laid.
It was started by those of mature personal and
Christian character, and experience in teaching;
and was from the first fostered by the church
and pastor. And unlike the earlier individual
enterprises, and the first attempts in many
towns, it had no transition state to undergo; it
pursued the course originally adopted,—only
gaining new wisdom by experience, and taking
advantage of the progress of light and knowledge.

But in pursuing its well defined objects, it
was now to occupy a new position and to realize
important and striking results.

The extensive revival of religion in the church
and congregation in 1830, had an intimate relation to the Sabbath school, both as cause and
effect. It could not but exert a marked influence in raising the standard of study and
instruction, and giving a higher tone of spiritual life to teachers and pupils. The enlightening Spirit disclosed new methods and ends of
labor; and the renewed heart, glowing with the
love of Christ, joyfully accepted the new and
congenial duties.

And this revival had special significance as a
test of Sabbath school instruction; as a seal of
God's favor on the study of His Word. "Ye

shall know them by their fruits." It was the time of the ingathering of harvest. Some "first fruits" had been gathered earlier. Eight of those connected with the Sabbath school had been hopefully converted in previous years. But now the seed sown brought forth abundantly "after his kind." Of the one hundred and forty-two who united with the church in this and the following years, as the direct result of this season of interest, sixty-six had been teachers or pupils.

From this time forward our Sabbath school has new points of interest, and new and wider elements of power. It henceforth became the dispenser as well as the receiver of good. It took in hand its own enterprises, which aimed at results beyond itself. The spirit of Christian charity once enkindled, gives birth to the spirit of true benevolence, which in its turn awakens and fosters the spirit of missions. As piety can alone estimate its own worth, so it alone can measure its want, and see the motive to supply this want.

Two of the members of our Sabbath school were now preparing to go forth as missionaries to the heathen; carrying the fruits of Sabbath school instruction; carrying the fitness to teach which comes of diligent learning, and becoming a living bond of sympathy between the school and the darkened children of the East perishing for lack of the bread of life. Thus new channels of thought and interest were opened; thus inquiry was stimulated; thus Christian activity was concentrated on a well defined object; thus the reflex influence of fourteen years came laden with blessings, and faith and hope and sight were made partakers of the present joy and were quickened for the labors of the future.

1830.

The Sabbath school was opened at the usual time in the spring of this year, under its former officers and teachers. During the spring and summer it held its sessions in the Town House. When the new meeting-house of the Hollis Evangelical Society was completed the school moved into the vestry; and now, for the first time in its history, it found a place of meeting both convenient and comfortable. From this time onward the Sabbath school was kept through the entire year.

1831.

In the spring of 1831 the Sabbath school was re-organized. C. F. W. Parkhurst was chosen Secretary, and from this date records more or less full have been kept.

Deacon Luther Haven was appointed Superintendent. The teachers were E. M. Capen, Elihu White, Jr., Calvin Shepard, Jr., C. F. W. Parkhurst, E. H. Warren, Alexander Abbott, Curtis Parker, W. P. Temple, Mrs. Eunice Capen, Sally Jones, Catherine Parker, Eliza C. Abbott, Emily S. Bell, Lucy C. Bent, Almira Walker, Eliza Wenzell, Eliza Ann Parker, Ann Maria Buckminster, Emily Parker, Asenath F. Eaton, Emily Johnson, Sarah Johnson, Abby H. Forrister, Mary W. Boynton, Harriet N. Shepard. More than half of these had been pupils in the school in previous years. The number of scholars was two hundred and fifty-four, of whom one hundred were adults.

THE SABBATH SCHOOL SOCIETY.

It appears that a Society—rather informal—was formed as early as 1818. Probably the only organization was a request from the Superintendent and teachers to Solomon Fay, that he would act as Secretary, to make out and keep a register of the names and recitations of the scholars. He had a natural taste, and thorough qualifications for this work, as the register will show. After his decease in 1820, probably no one was found with like qualifications, who was specially interested in the school, and no regular records were kept for several years. But the form and name of the Society were continued, as is shown by the inscription in the books given as presents to the scholars for good conduct and good recitations. It comprised only the teachers; and the only action taken was the annual election of Superintendent, who was also Secretary and Treasurer.

In 1825, the Massachusetts Sabbath School Union was formed, (embracing the Baptist and Congregational denominations,) consisting of superintendents, teachers, and earnest friends of the cause, with a view, among other things, "to stimulate and encourage each other in the moral and religious instruction of children and others." This Union formed a nucleus around which the Sabbath schools gathered; and by an interchange of views, and comparison of plans, and collating particular results, more of uniformity and systematic management was introduced, and a common mode of conducting the schools was adopted.

A Society, auxiliary to this State Society, was formed in Framingham, as early as 1826. As the constitution and records are lost, no specific account of the working of the Society can be given. Probably it adopted substantially the method hitherto pursued in the school; only acting as a recognized head, and doing by formal vote, what had been done by common consent.

In 1831, in order to infuse new life into the school, and enlist more general support, the constitution of the Society was revised, by a committee appointed for the purpose. The committee consisted of Deacon John Temple, Patten Johnson, Ezra Hemenway, Deacon Luther Haven, and Edmund M. Capen.

By the new constitution, the Society still continued auxiliary to the State Society. As stated in the records, the special objects to be kept in view were "to provide a suitable place for the instruction of children and youth on the Sabbath, and to raise funds for the establishment of a library for the use of the school." All interested in the object, by signing their names, and paying twenty-five cents annually, became members, and could vote in the choice of officers. The officers of the Society appointed the teachers; and the teachers nominated a Superintendent, who must be confirmed by the officers. No book could be introduced into the school without the consent of the officers. The number of members enrolled was one hundred and thirty-nine, embracing the most active members of the church.

The general mode of conducting the exercises was, 1. The school was opened with singing and prayer. 2. The teachers heard the lessons of their respective classes. 3. Exercises closed by singing. 4. On the last Sabbath of the month, the lessons recited during the month were publicly reviewed by the Superintendent, or some one appointed by the Directors. 5. It was the duty of the Superintendent, on all ordinary occasions, to request those who were connected with the school to lead in devotion, and take a part in the various other exercises.

In 1842, the constitution was again revised. Committee, Rev. David Brigham, J. J. Marshall and Marshall Conant. The connection with the State Society was severed. The whole control of the Sabbath school was vested in the teachers and those pupils who were twenty-one years of age and upwards. None others could become members of the Society. The church was no longer to have any voice in the management of the school. How the teachers were appointed, does not appear. The number of members enrolled was thirty-four.

In 1852, a committee, consisting of Carlos Slafter, Deacon E. M. Capen, C. F. W. Parkhurst, Deacon Eben Eaton, and Andrew Coolidge, was appointed to examine and revise the constitution of the Society.

The most important change is indicated in article 3: "This Society shall consist of the members of the church, and of such other individuals as shall sign the constitution,"—thus restoring the school to its first position as the child of the church. The Superintendent was chosen by the Society. The board of officers appointed the teachers. The only rule adopted for conducting the school was, "The exercises shall be opened with prayer, and closed with singing." All other parts of the service were left to the discretion of the Superintendent. This constitution has continued in force to the present day.

Without instituting any comparisons, which might do injustice, it is probably safe to say, that the enlightened sentiment of the real friends and supporters of the Sabbath school has settled down to the conclusion, that the Sabbath school must hold an intimate relation to the church; that all its principles of action must be in harmony with, and directly promotive of, the doctrines and fellowship, and piety of the church; that in reality it must be under the watch and care of the church. The formal and recognized relation between the two must be such, that the church *is held responsible* for the conduct and results of the Sabbath school. So intimately connected are both with the religious interests of society; so potent the influences which cluster around each, and extend to the families, and fireside counsels, and home altars, that any antagonism in essentials is fatal to one or the other or both. Indifference on the part of the church will prove a fetter on the progress of the Sabbath school. As the mother to her child, so the church must guard and foster and nurture, and cherish in prayer and faith and love, the Sabbath school.

ADULT DEPARTMENT.

Early in the year 1831, an *adult department* was organized, separate from the juvenile department, or Sabbath school proper. It met in the audience-room of the church. It numbered about one hundred, and was divided into classes of suitable size. Patten Johnson was chosen Superintendent, and instructed a class. The same question-book was used as in the juvenile school.

This department was kept up as a distinct school for five or six years. Patten Johnson was Superintendent till 1835. Deacon Ezra Hemenway was Superintendent from that date till 1837 or '38,—when the two schools were merged in one.

In the opinion of those who took part in the work, a separate department for adults worked well, and accomplished its objects successfully. It is easy to see the advantages of such a department, in the general mode of management, and adaptation of means. It is difficult to meet the wants of youthful and mature minds by any one method of instruction. The statement and illustration of religious doctrine needs to be varied to suit their different points of view; and it requires much skill and knowledge of human nature to adapt general remarks equally to both old and young. And in awakening interest, and stimulating inquiry, different methods are necessary. This is in part accomplished by classification,—each teacher adapting himself to the peculiar age and character of his class. But all general exercises will fail to interest equally the two extremes. And in fact, the Superintendent, from the real necessity of the case, will lay his plans, and conduct the school, with almost exclusive reference to the children.

On the other hand, it should be said, the moral power of a school is greatly increased by the presence of parents, and the aged church-members. Their presence is itself an incitement, and a restraint. The lesson has a higher value to a child, if he knows that his father, and perhaps his grandfather are studying and reciting it with him. The Word of God has higher significance and more sacredness, when age and wisdom and scholarship gather with infancy around it for instruction. If the child sees the mature Christian thus earnestly searching the Scriptures, to find "eternal life," a sense of reality—of weighty concern—of immediate obligation—attaches to the study ; a sense of the difficulties of the Christian life is gained ;

a consciousness of the need of more than human aid and strength,—of the help of divine grace, is awakened ; and thus the thoughts and purposes are turned to Him, who is " the Way and the Truth and the Life."

One most important result which followed the establishment of this separate department, was *the enlistment for life* of the fathers and mothers in the Sabbath school. Now, after thirty years, they—the survivors—are all in their places in the classes, and as deeply interested as then in the study of the Bible. The mantle of those who are " taken up" falls on some one who at once fills the vacant seat. It is a most interesting fact, that the proportion between adults and children—one hundred to one hundred and sixty-six—has been kept up without essential variation from 1831 to the present time. In 1859, the numbers were, ninety-nine adults, and one hundred sixty-three children.

And the first thing which strikes a stranger on entering our school, is the crowded adult classes. All the eagerness and all the zest of youth are manifest in their attitude and manner, as they scan the Sacred Oracles, and seek for the mind of the Spirit. And the children of these parents are uniformly punctual and constant in attendance; while the children of absent parents are irregular, and readily find excuses for tardiness and absence.

Some of these adult classes use the common question-book of the school, and some are Bible classes,—the choice being generally left to themselves.

One teacher, Mr. P. H. Vose, has had charge of a class without interruption, for thirty-three years. And although in that time there have been seventy different pupils connected with the class, one of the original members now remains.

INFANT DEPARTMENT.

Infant classes, in connection with, or as a part of the Sabbath school, began to be formed as early as 1827–28. The specific object was to gather by themselves a considerable number of children, too young to study the regular lessons from the question-books, and teach them the Lord's prayer, hymns, and Bible verses, and exercise them in singing devotional songs, and other general performances of a religious nature.

The first infant class in our school, was established by Miss Emeline Stone, in 1832. It was conducted successfully by her for a number of years. Her successors have been, Martha Ann Abbott, Abby H. Forrister, Susan M. Abbott, Emeline Hemenway, Mrs. T. Forrister, Mrs. O. Bennett, Mrs. Jones, Augusta March, Harriett March, C. E. Burnap, Harriett Williams, F. Williams, Lucy P. Brown, Mary Marshall, Grace Parker.

It has been till the present year, a separate department, meeting in a room by itself. Two classes, one of boys, and one of girls, have been graduated from it into the Sabbath school, every spring. The average number in this department, for a series of years has been forty.

This is an interesting, and an important branch of the Sabbath school. Probably it is the most difficult class to teach, requiring talent and tact of a high order, and especially a thorough knowledge of child nature, and a loving, Christian heart. Quiet deportment, and a good degree of interested attention, are necessary to be secured, without great pressure of visible restraint, or show of authority. No exercise should be introduced for the sake of mere amusement. The sacredness of the day should be reciprocated in the feelings awakened, and the impressions made by the lessons and songs. All parts of the service should be adapted to children, and designed to implant and nurture in them a reverence for God, a sacred regard for holy things, and a dread of sin. And it is ever to be borne in mind, that it is not the amount of truth taught,—not the repetition of words,—not the process of reasoning,—not the urgent advice and warning; but *the spirit* in which instruction is given, and *the impression* made on the heart of the child, which are vital, and tell on the life. The winning look of tenderness and sympathy is remembered, long after the words are forgotten. A devout spirit and a likeness to Jesus in the teacher, will attract the young to Him better than persuasive appeals. And if one clear idea of the nature of holiness is imparted, and one true desire for a holy heart is awakened in the child, the teaching is effective.

Nowhere is there a greater liability to commit errors, and by an injudicious presentation of religious truth, poison the mind for life; and on the other hand, nowhere does the " meekness of wisdom," and the exhibition of true piety, more surely bear much fruit. If for any reason, the mother *will excuse herself* from the duty God has laid upon her, to teach the infant lips to lisp prayer and praise to him, and to turn the first thoughts and purposes of life to the Saviour, then let this department of Sabbath schools be sacredly cherished.

SABBATH SCHOOL CONCERT.

The Sabbath school concert was observed in our school as early as 1831.

The idea of this concert was evidently borrowed from the missionary concert, which had been observed in the churches since 1813. It recognized the vital importance which attached to the Sabbath school as a means of religious education; and the duty of the church to offer special prayer for the divine direction and blessing. At first, it was a *concert of prayer*. And the intention evidently was, that the members of the church generally should gather with the teachers and scholars, and thus publicly identify themselves with the cause.

This, its original purpose, and the method by which its founders sought to accomplish the object, are to be borne in mind whenever we would estimate the value of this concert, or trace its history. The marked favor of God on the Sabbath school, in the revivals which visited the churches in 1830, not only indicated its value as a means of grace, but clearly evinced the duty of supplicating God's special blessing on the institution continually. It was made evident that this was one of the chosen means by which He was building up and strengthening His people in intelligence, and active benevolence, as well as in numbers. And the great good which had resulted from the missionary concert, in imparting intelligent views of the work of missions, and uniting the hearts of Christians in true sympathy with the work, and in the common offerings laid on the altar, — naturally suggested a similar monthly meeting to gain knowledge, and awaken interest, and unite all in offerings, and in intercessions for the divine favor on the Sabbath school.

When first established, and for many years, the concert was observed on the evening of the second Sabbath in each month. Usually a carefully prepared address was delivered by the pastor, or some invited stranger, or one of the officers, on a topic directly related to Sabbath schools.

In those years it was kept up with varied interest. Sometimes the vestry would be well filled, and "the spirit of grace and supplications" would be poured upon His people. Sometimes only the school would be present; and the Superintendent and teachers would yield to discouragement. The annual report of the school for 1837, says: "The Sabbath school concert is observed, though with a slight degree of interest on the part of the church,"—indicating that the officers of the school felt the need of the hearty co-operation and united prayers of professed Christians.

In 1842, the time of holding the concert was changed. It then was made to take the place of the regular school recitations on the second Sabbath noon of each month, and was conducted by the officers of the school. It was conducted much like an ordinary religious meeting,—singing, prayers, and addresses alternating, only each part of the exercises had a special bearing on the school.

The concert has been regularly observed till the present time, though the mode of its management has greatly varied in different years. Perhaps the most marked difference between the present and former methods of conducting it, is, that now the pupils are relied on to give character and interest to the exercises, rather than the officers and the church. Perhaps now the custom is general, to have some system of Scripture recitations,—varied to suit circumstances, and the discretion of the Superintendent. In some instances, an historical fact, as the deluge, the offering of Isaac, the captivities, the crucifixion, the conversion of

Paul; or some topic, as the Sabbath, baptism, is announced, and each scholar is expected to commit a verse relating to the fact or topic. In others, a word is given out, and the verses to be recited are to contain this word. In some cases a letter is named as the initial of the selected passages. Sometimes a teacher is designated to write an essay, or historical sketch, or brief discussion of the doctrine or topic or fact given out. In some schools, individual pupils are called by name, and rise and repeat their verse. In others, a class is designated, and the class rise, and each member in turn recites his verse or paragraph.

The success of any method depends on the ready and hearty zeal with which all co-operate and do their part. Probably it is the experience of superintendents generally, that to awaken and sustain an interest in the concert, —to make it really profitable to the school, is one of the most difficult of his—often—difficult duties.

BENEVOLENT CONTRIBUTIONS.

Intimately associated with the rise of the Sabbath school concert, was the custom of taking up regular monthly contributions for benevolent objects, in the Sabbath school. Indeed this was a part of the original plan. Effectual prayer and active benevolence are always associated. It is difficult to separate them. To supplicate God's blessing on a cause which demands action, individual or associated, implies a pledge to do what is requisite to further the cause; implies the consecration to Him of what means one possesses that are needed in advancing the cause.

Concerted prayer for the Sabbath school, by the church, was a pledge of effort and sacrifice in behalf of the Sabbath school. Gracious blessings received in answer to prayer and faithful labor, bound the recipients to requite those bestowed favors, by efforts to extend the advantages of Sabbath school instruction to the destitute. The love of Christ implanted in the heart prompts to Christ-like benevolence. It is but half of goodness to be good ; to do good, to impart to others what God so freely bestows, is the larger half of goodness itself. Selfishness *keeps* its treasures for their enjoyment; true goodness imparts them, in order to keep them. And the enjoyment of the Christian life consists essentially in offering that life a sacrifice for others.

"The grace of giving," is a beautiful trait of true childhood, as it is of true manhood. The trivial gift bestowed with generous impulses is most acceptable, and praiseworthy. The penny, which might have been expended for sweetmeats, bestowed with a look of love on the deserving poor; the little book, which is cherished for its own sake, and given for Christ's sake to a schoolmate who has no little books; the hour of play-time, devoted to reading the Bible to a blind neighbor;—these are not costly gifts; but they are precious beyond all price. They are the expression of traits which He loves who looketh on the heart. They are traits which our Saviour well delineates when he says, "Of such is the kingdom of heaven."

To cultivate this spirit of charity, should be one aim of all education; as the best success and the truest enjoyment of life are promoted by it. And to inculcate and develop this spirit should be a constant aim of Sabbath school instruction. It is the spirit of the whole Bible;

it is pre-eminently the spirit of the gospel. The love of God opens the heart; and the generous heart opens the hands; and the charity —small if the means are small, large if the means are large—bestowed for Christ's sake, and consecrated by prayer, returns from its mission, as an answer to that prayer, laden with sweet peace and hope to the soul.

It is only when this reflex influence of charity is rightly comprehended, that the essential need of bringing up children in the practice of self-denial, and in habits of a generous consideration of others, can be rightly comprehended, and that this means of the best moral culture will be thoughtfully improved by parents.

To contribute their little savings of money is the common mode of benevolence; though kind actions, and self-denial, and unsought sympathy, and the numerous ministrations of generous love, in the home, and the school, and in society, are alike valuable as gifts, and for the imparting and receiving of joy. What constitutes the essence of charity, is the cheerful and hearty bestowment on others of what is highly prized by us. God demanded of his chosen people of old the offering of the "*first-fruits*" of their fields and flocks, because they were the most needed and the most valuable to the possessor. He never accepts what is left, after all our wants are supplied; or what has no intrinsic value to us. And the offering of such things in charity brings no joy to the soul. Every gift, then, laid on the human or the divine altar, must needs be consecrated by love and prayer; and every gift must be in the best sense a sacrifice. Hence the appropriateness of a Sabbath school concert for prayer and benevolent contributions.

Regular contributions for benevolent objects were taken once a month, in our school, from the time when the Sabbath school concert was established. It has always been the avowed purpose to distribute the avails of these collections in promoting the cause of Sabbath schools. Some of the funds have been expended in making the superintendents and teachers life members of the Sabbath School Society, or the American S. S. Union; some portions have been spent in the purchase of libraries for new and destitute schools at the West, in Iowa and Minnesota. Twenty dollars were sent to Mrs. Schneider of Aintab, a former pupil and teacher of the school, for the benefit of Sabbath schools in Syria.

To 1858, the amount annually realized from the monthly collections averaged $25. In

1859, the plan was started of taking up *penny contributions* on each Sabbath. The result has been a large increase in the amount collected. For the nine years that this plan has been in operation, the amount has averaged $65 per annum. This method is still practised. The giving of a penny is entirely voluntary; but the number usually falls very little below the total number of teachers and scholars present on the day.

THE LIBRARY.

The first collection of books for the use of the school has been noticed. After the reorganization in 1831, the library became an important means of keeping up an interest, and drawing in pupils. And at this date, a large number of books designed for children, had been published.

In 1830, the library comprised one hundred and thirty-three volumes. Seventy-two volumes were added in 1831 : one hundred and twenty-two volumes were added in 1832 ; eighty-five volumes in 1833. In this year a thorough overhauling of the library was made ; lost books were stricken from the catalogue ; some re-bound, and all re-numbered. And the renovated library was found to contain two hundred and sixty-nine volumes.

Two hundred volumes were added in 1835. In 1845, $75 was expended for new books. In 1856, a new library was purchased, and a part of the old one sent to a school at the West.

In 1859, the whole number of books was four hundred and seventy-seven. In 1860, $120 was expended to purchase books for the library.

In 1865, the number of volumes in the library was five hundred and forty-eight.

In 1868, a part of the library was sent to Minnesota, and the sum of $200 was raised to add new books, making the number now in the library five hundred and fifty-three.

Mode of managing the distribution of Books.—A printed catalogue is allowed to each family connected with the school. This list gives the number of pages, as well as the title of the book. Blank cards are furnished to each pupil, containing his name and number, and ruled with spaces for the title and number of the book wanted; on which each is expected to designate several books, so that in case he does not get his first choice at once, he may receive a second choice, and have a chance to get the other soon. The number of the book given him is checked on the card, and also on the librarian's corresponding list,—the check to be erased when the book is returned. Books are given out on each Sabbath, one volume only to a pupil; and he is not entitled to another till the first is returned.

TABLE OF STATISTICS.

1818. Number of teachers, 10; number of pupils, 142; average attendance, 70.

1831. Number of teachers, 34; number of pupils, 254.

1836. Number of teachers, 30; number of pupils, 260, of whom 100 were adults.

1840. Twenty-seven members of the Sabbath school united with the church, by profession.

1859. Number of teachers, 22; number of pupils, 262, of which 78 are between 15 and 30 years; 21 are over 50 years. Sixty of the pupils, and all the teachers are members of the church.

1861. Number of teachers, 25; number of pupils, 265; average attendance, 167; number over 15 years of age, 154; members of the church, 108.

1863. Whole number of pupils, 272; 114 are members of the church, of whom 36 have indulged hope this year.

1864. Fourteen pupils professed religion.

1865. Number of teachers, 26; number of pupils, 263; average attendance, 165.

1868. Twenty members of the Sabbath school are indulging the Christian hope, since the beginning of the year.

LIST OF SUPERINTENDENTS.

Deacon LUTHER HAVEN, 1816–19, 1831, 5 years.
ABNER STONE, 1820–22, ... 3 years.
Deacon EBEN EATON, 1823–30, 1832,
   1837–45, ... 18 years.
CALVIN SHEPARD, Jr., 1833, . . . 1 year.
C. F. W. PARKHURST, 1834–36, . . 3 years.
JOHN J. MARSHALL, 1846, 1847, . . 2 years.
PATTEN JOHNSON, 1848–51, . . . 4 years.
CARLOS SLAFTER, 1852, ... 1 year.
B. K. HAVEN, 1853, ... 1 year.
Deacon ANDREW COOLIDGE, 1854, 1857, 2 years.
B. F. WILSON, 1855, 1856, ... 2 years.
Deacon G. W. BIGELOW, 1858–63, . 6 years.
Deacon WILLIAM F. EAMES, 1864–67, 4 years.
Deacon ANDREW COOLIDGE, 1868.

1868.

OFFICERS OF THE SABBATH SCHOOL.

Superintendent, Deacon Andrew Coolidge. *First Vice-President*, Sewall Fisher. *Second Vice-President*, John L. Sanger. *Treasurer*, George A. Thompson. *Secretary*, George M. Amsden. *Librarians*, Henry F. White, George D. Bigelow.

Teacher of Infant Class, Grace Parker.

Class: Cora I. Lamson, Susan M. Young, Theophilus H. Root, Frank Gibbs, Arthur K. Stone, Neverson Hemenway, Emma E. Hagar, Minnie N. Hagar, Frank E. Rice, Alice Hastings, George H. Taylor, Willie F. Hosmer, Albert J. Haven, Katie T. Blake, Gracia D. Blake, Willie Harrington, Frank A. Young, Walter W. Eames, Nattie M. Ladd, Wallace Kendall, Laura A. Sanderson, Charles Otis.

Teacher of Bible Class, Susan Rebecca Eaton.

Class: Mrs. A. B. Tufts, Mrs. E. Conant, Mrs. Grace G. Barnard, Mrs. Hitty Gates, Mrs. A. M. Parsons, Mrs. J. A. Hammond, Mrs. J. M. Harrington, Mrs. E. Hemenway, Mrs. E. Jones, Mrs. S. Fisher, Mrs. Laura Amsden, Mrs. Leander Barber, Mrs. Mary Ann Smith, Mrs. John Fenton, Mrs. Clara W. Morse, M.

Thompson, E. Thompson, Susan E. Edmands, Mary Cutting, E. Bailey, Helen Barnard, Caroline E. Burnap, Mrs. C. Sanderson, Mrs. M. M. Coolidge, Mrs. T. Garratt, Sally Jones, Mrs. C. Baker, Sarah A. Temple, Mrs. Ellen B. Fairbank.

Teacher, Doctor T. D. Chamberlain.

Class: Benj. K. Haven, George Nourse, John Cutting, George A. Thompson, J. T. Forrister, Frederic Coe, Leander Barber, Edmond M. Capen, Josiah Gibbs, John L. Sanger, George M. Amsden, George W. Bigelow, A. D. Cloyes, Charles Trowbridge.

Teacher, J. D. Chamberlain.

Class: Mrs. Harriett Rice, Mrs. N. Hosmer, Mrs. H. Sanger, Mrs. J. Gibbs, Mrs. A. Woods, Mrs. P. H. Vose, Mrs. A. Pratt, C. E. Lincoln.

Teacher, Benj. F. Wilson. (P. H. Vose.)

Class: Mrs. E. G. Eaton, Mrs. Mary Stearns, Mrs. Harriett Cloyes, Mrs. G. J. Childs, Mrs. E. Rice, Mrs. Edwin Hastings, Mrs. T. Forrister, Mrs. G. A. Trowbridge, Mrs. Henry Eames, Mrs. Luther Eames, Mrs. John Forrister, Mrs. Curtis Belcher, Mrs. Ellis D. Hall, Mrs. D. F. Chadwick, Martha Merriam.

Teacher, William Symmes.

Class: A. Sidney Bull, Henry E. Warren, Richard Briggs, Frederic Coe, Jr., Nathan

Gates, Charles Smyth, Joseph Weston, Edwin Walkup, A. Cutting, T. Eaton, Ellis Hall, Edw. Dodge.

Teacher, Mrs. J. Mann.

Class: George D. Bigelow, George Edw. West, Charles Parsons, Lewis Russell, Frederic B. Horne, C. Sidney Eames, Alphonso Capen, Henry F. White.

Teacher, Mrs. Mary B. Temple.

Class: Ann Maria Cutting, Sarah Cutting, Susan Williams, Nettie Barnard, Carrie A. West, Sarah A. Faucett, Abby Pratt, Maria Pratt.

Teacher, Mrs. S. N. Brewer.

Class: Mary E. Temple, Mary Sanderson, M. Isabel Eames, Abby Russell, Ann M. Brigham, Nancy Walkup, Ella W. Hastings, Hattie E. Smith, Kittie Otis.

Teacher, Sewall Fisher.

Class: Lizzie Moore, Mary Briggs, Hattie E. Rice, Lizzie Haven, Anna L. Sanger, Fanny Eames, Anna L. West.

Teacher, Irene Poole.

Class: Mary L. B. Esty, Lizzie Hastings, Cora Barrett, Anna Gibbs, Eva Bisbee.

Teacher, Emma Clark.

Class: Jenny Rice, Jenny Livermore, Minnie Woods, Blanche Walkup, Lizzie Blake, Emma E. Gates.

Teacher, Ann Maria Eaton.

Class: J. Ada Smith, Susan E. Cloyes, Clara Walkup, Ella Hemenway, Justina Ware, Addie Lamson, Emma Eaton, Ada R. Smith, Cora Moore, Ella Chadwick.

Teacher, Anna L. Hastings.

Class: Augusta Barber, Alice West, Emily Cloyes, Jessie Walkup, Ella Forrister, Abby Wheeler, Ada Partridge, Fanny Hastings.

Teacher, Lizzie Stone.

Class: Hattie Jewell, Ada Washburn, Jenny Hastings, M. Ella Smith, G. Winch, Ella F. Belcher.

Teacher, (Sarah J. Russell.) Georgiana Barnard.

Class: Willis Rowell, John H. Temple, Charles Trowbridge, Frank Rowell, Horace Chamberlain, Frank A. Walkup, Andrew Belcher.

Teacher, Martha Bailey.

Class: Waldo Howe, Franklin Howe, Arthur Coe, Henry Coe, Eddie Harrington, Roger Sherman, Waldo Johnson.

Teacher, Abby Kelley.

Class: William Trowbridge, Granville Forrister, Thomas West, Thomas Hastings, Frank Haven, Charles Williams, Frederic Esty.

Teacher, Flora Williams.

Class: Eddy White, Josiah Hastings, Charles Esty, Enos H. Bigelow, Frederic Hosmer, Allston Swan, Charles Taylor.

Teacher, Ellen M. Moore.

Class: Edward C. Smith, Alexander N. Esty, Harry E. Swan, Elbridge C. Barber, Gardner P. Hastings, Willie H. Lamson, Frank Coe.

Teacher, Mrs. Abby H. F. Russell.

Class: Sarah Gibbs, Angeline A. Chadwick, L. Isabel Chadwick, Mary Cutting, Abby Cutting, Mary E. Eaton, Hannah Sanderson.

Teacher, Ellen Stone.

Class: Lizzie A. Root, Georgianna Harrington, Elberta Hemenway, Mary A. Eames, Lizzie Bigelow, Kittee Esty, Mira Hagar, Jenny Kendall, Emma Stone, Nettie Stone, Jennie Otis, Lizzie Otis, Mary Parker.

Teacher, Louisa A. Eames.

Class: Edgar Harrington, Charles Lamson, Joseph Weston, Fred. W. Young, Andrew Belcher.

Teacher, Anna E. Johnson.

Class: Josephine Bennett, and six others.

The school meets in the audience-room of the church, on Sabbath noons; each session continuing forty-five minutes. The exercises are opened with prayer and singing, and recitations from the Psalms, in concert; and closed with singing.

All the officers and teachers are members of the church; and eighty of the pupils are professors or have indulged hope in the recent revival.

Two of the classes are *Bible classes*. There are five adult classes. The question-book now in use is "Clark's Questions on the great Truths of the Bible,"—the adults using No. 3, the school proper using No. 2, and the infant class using No. 1.

One of the teachers, Mrs. Abby H. F. Russell, and one of the pupils, Mrs. Grace G. Barnard, were members of the class which met in the Academy Hall September 8, 1816. Deacon E. M. Capen, now in the adult class, was a teacher in the school in 1819. Thus is the half century made a reality to us, by the living chain which connects its two extremes; and thus is the proof furnished that the principles in which the institution was founded have not needed change, nor grown old, nor obsolete. The same Holy Word is now the subject of study, and the guide to Truth, and the lamp to show the path to Life and Rest. Depending on the same divine aid, the teachers now labor in hope, and the scholars listen to the precepts of

Him who said, "Suffer the little children to come unto me; for of such is the kingdom of heaven."

Perhaps the true relation of the Sabbath school to the church, is more obvious—though not more real—when it is seen gathered in the same sanctuary. The people gather in the morning, and are led in worship, and in sacred song, and Scripture meditation, by the pastor; with a brief interval, a large portion of the same congregation are earnestly engaged with their teachers, in studying "the great truths of the Bible," and in prayer and praise; then, after another short recess, the assembly again appears before God, lifting up the heart and voice in supplications and praises, and inquiring of the Sacred Oracles. It is a common pursuit of a common end. The church provides for and watches over the school; and the school is auxiliary to the church; is in nurture for the church. They are identified in interest, and the school is eventually to become the church. And the church discharges its duty to the school only when it cherishes and supports it with its whole heart.

And very grateful is the sight of this garden of the Lord; very precious are the offerings of the "first fruits" laid on His altar; very cheering are the hopes which God's promises insure. "They that seek me early shall find me." "Blessed are they that sow beside all waters."

And very striking is it, and emblematic of our common sinfulness, to see the infant of days and the hoary head, bowing together at the same mercy-seat! Very beautiful, and emblematic of the full provisions of the atonement and mediation of the Son of God, and the blessings in store for the believing soul, is it, when the child and the parent and the grandparent—he that is born in the house, and the stranger—meet on a common level,—hearing the words of the great Teacher; looking to the same precious blood for redemption; owning the same gracious covenant; and, "if children, then heirs: heirs of God, and joint-heirs with Christ."

And from this review of fifty-two years, what is the practical lesson taught? How is the Sabbath school to be made most effective for its true ends? By Christian love, and Christian fidelity. Various methods have been devised to awaken interest, and promote efficient and harmonious work in the school; but the true secret may be summed up in a single expression,—*deep-toned piety* in the officers and teachers. They will gain the eye and the ear, and the heart of their pupils, when they come to the school with their own hearts glowing with the love of God, and alive to the worth of the soul.

In Memoriam.

The sketches which follow, of four of the founders of the Sabbath school, can scarcely claim the title of memoirs; they are rather tributes of affectionate remembrance to former teachers by surviving pupils,—most of the materials being gathered from the memories of those who were members of the school during the first six years of its existence.

The purpose in publishing these tributes, is, to show that Christian principle, and faithful Christian labor, even in a narrow and humble sphere, result in great good, and bring much honor to Christ.

ABNER STONE.

Mr. Stone may properly be called one of the originators of the Sabbath school,—though the plan was suggested by, and the first class was gathered by ladies. He gave his sanction and support to the movement, and took part in instructing a class of boys from the outset.

He belonged to a family bearing an honored name in Framingham. He was carefully trained in childhood by an excellent mother, who lived to see the precious fruit of her counsel and influence.

He was educated at the Framingham Academy; going through a thorough course of English studies, and making considerable progress in the Latin language, with a view of pursuing a collegiate education, which plan he subsequently abandoned. It was this academic course which fitted him for the prominent position he held as a teacher in the Sabbath school. The habits he had acquired, of careful thought, and close investigation, and logical reasoning, prepared him for a profitable study of the Scriptures, and gave him aptness in proposing questions, and solving difficulties.

He had to struggle, through life, with a constitutional bashfulness, which kept him silent in public, before a large audience; but before his class, as in all more private consultations, he was collected, and could give fit expression to acceptable thoughts; and his efficiency and promptness in acting, where deeds could speak as well as words, compensated, in a great degree, for his constrained silence.

Mr. Stone was hopefully converted in the revival of 1814–15. At this time he had reached mature life,—being thirty-seven years old, which will account in part for the fact that he could not overcome the early habit of shrinking from public speaking, even in religious meetings,—though his growth in the Christian graces was rapid and marked.

He entered into the work of the Christian life with his whole heart, as his only way of "redeeming the time." Clear in his views of Scripture doctrines; deeply conscientious; calm in judgment and broad in his observations, his counsels were entitled to, and always received great weight. And his firmness of purpose, when the path of duty was made plain, made him a pillar in the church. So reliable and earnest was he as a church member, and so judicious and active a supporter of the Sabbath school, as of every good work, that when the new church was formed at Saxonville, with which movement he was from location identified, the pastor of the mother church remarked, on his leaving, that "his right arm was cut off."

He possessed a symmetrical and well-balanced character. No one trait was prominent; and there was no essential trait lacking, to cause an observable deficiency. If anything impressed a close observer more than another, in his character, it was his guileless transparency. You could see through him; you felt, when in his presence, that there was no dissembling, and no concealment. The thorough subjugation of his mental and moral powers to the law of Christ, after his conversion; the singular truthfulness of his nature, which showed itself in all his life; the subdued yet earnest and devout spirit which was a part of his daily walk and ways, were always apparent,—not because he sought to exhibit them, but because they were his moral life; because they constituted himself.

And these powers and graces were set apart to Christ and his church. This was the one aim of his public Christian course. And this singleness of purpose, coupled with a devout spirit, and truthful nature, gave an even tenor to his life, and consecrated that life to "whatsoever things are true, whatsoever things are honest, whatsoever things are just, whatsoever things are pure, whatsoever things are lovely, whatsoever things are of good report." If he did not give expression to the ecstasies of Christian enjoyment, and the more demonstrative experiences, he could speak of the love of Christ, and a well-grounded hope of pardon. If he never rose high in influence with his fellow men, he was never without influence; and this influence was beneficent, was conservative, was attractive,—was of a kind to win men to the pleasant paths of wisdom and piety. For piety in him, was a genial, inspiring power; pervading words and deeds; giving color to opinions and plans; moulding social as well as religious character. It led him to sympathize with the sick and sorrowing, and to devote what time and skill he had to their relief, cheerfully, in season and out of season. Many a tear of gratitude, taking the place of tears of sorrow and suffering, has been his tribute and reward.

His reverence for the Sabbath, and love of the sanctuary were marked traits of Mr. Stone's character. Till the age of fifty-five, he resided three miles from the church, but his place in the house of God on the Sabbath was rarely vacant; and none engaged in worship, and received the word of life more eagerly and gratefully than he. When the church near his home at Saxonville was formed in 1833, none prized the privilege of ready access to Christian ordinances more than he; and none more faithfully attended on all religious services. One who was his pastor, says: "My intercourse with Mr. Stone for the ten years of my ministry there, was one of unbroken confidence and felicity. His general simplicity, and I may say transparency of character, were always a matter of intense study with me; and to this day, are my highest idea of a gospel, Scripture righteousness.

"In every question of obvious duty, we always knew where to find Mr. Stone.

"So settled and principled were his ideas of sanctuary ordinances; so constant his appearance in the house of God, that we did not need to ask if something serious was the matter, when his seat was left vacant. Indeed I have always felt, and often quoted his case as one of God's genuine household; not from any special measure of gift, but from *fulfilling in the best sense the measure that was given him;* fulfilling the stewardship of God's trust in the best intents of probation."

In personal appearance, Mr. Stone was tall, and slightly stooping, as of a man not in high health. His features were regular, and his countenance wore the expression of benignity and gentle thoughts. Those who were his pupils in the Sabbath school remember with grateful interest, his pleasant voice, and the quiet way in which he proposed questions and gave instructions. Though not awed by his presence, they were attracted by his manner. There was an evident sincerity, and simple earnestness, which touched the heart; and the clearness of his statements of truth carried conviction to the understanding. Thus his influence over his class was constraining rather than impulsive; and the effect of his teaching was permanent. He is cherished by them with warm regard.

By his fellow teachers he was held in high esteem. Though not apt to obtrude his opinions, he always had an opinion, and was ready to give it, when the case required; and it was uniformly found worthy of respect. He looked at questions of duty and plans of action, from a practical standpoint; and his mind was remarkably free from bias or prejudice. The law of love was in his heart; and he seemed never to lose sight of the fact that he was one of Christ's disciples. And when plans of action were to be carried out, and wise counsels to be transformed into deeds, none was found more efficient than he. Quietly, but directly, and promptly, he did his part. And when the duty was well discharged, and good results achieved, he was not careful to claim any of the honor.

He was Superintendent of the Sabbath school for two or three years, though he took the place with some reluctance; and discharged its duties, as he did all duties, with singleness of purpose, as unto Christ.

He lived to see the church and Sabbath

school send out two considerable colonies, which grew into important centres of influence. And at his death, the mother church and the school were both stronger, and had larger numbers enrolled, than before sending forth the colonies. "There is that scattereth, and yet increaseth."

He died February, 1859, at the ripe age of eighty-one. The sweet savor of a gentle, devout, godly life attaches to his memory.

ABAGAIL BENT.

Of the three young ladies—Abagail Bent, Martha Trowbridge and Mary Brown—who unitedly started the Sabbath school, it may be difficult to decide which performed the more important part of the work. But to Miss Bent belongs the honor of taking the lead in suggesting, and carrying into operation the devised plan. Indeed she was by nature fitted to be a leader in new enterprises. Of quick discernment, and active temperament; with her acquisitions always at command, and self-reliant; she was ready to act, when others had only possessed themselves of the means for forming a wise judgment. And as the goodness of her motive was unquestioned, and her plans feasible, it was common for them to be substantially adopted.

She had seen the working of a Sabbath school in Bath, N. H., while engaged in teaching a public school in that village, in previous years. She may have assisted in this school, as the Rev. Mr. Sutherland, its founder, was a valued friend of her family. She at least had a knowledge of his method of conducting his class; which could not fail to be of service in the opening of our Sabbath school.

Miss Bent was left a half-orphan, by the death of her mother, when eight years old. She had good advantages for education, at the Framingham Academy, and at Mrs. Rowson's school in Newton. After completing her studies, she taught school during the summer months, for several years. She made a profession of religion in 1805, when twenty-three years old. Her thoughts were specially directed to her spiritual interests, by a sermon preached by Rev. John Brewer, in Dr. Kellogg's pulpit. "She went home from meeting under deep conviction of sin,—feeling that she was lost,—but unable to find a Saviour. She tried to pray; but the door of mercy seemed to be shut." Her distress and darkness lasted for a considerable time, when she was enabled to cast herself unconditionally on the mercy of God in Jesus Christ. Then light and peace came and filled her soul, as it had been full of anguish and forebodings.

This *true and deep conviction of sin*, which she experienced, and which preceded her Christian hope, had an important influence on her subsequent Christian life. Probably it is the common experience of Christ's disciples, that the deeper their sense of the guilt of sin, the truer their joy at deliverance from its curse; the more they realize their helpless and undone condition by nature, the more they appreciate the recovering grace of God; the clearer they discover the plague of their own hearts, the more attractive appears that holiness without which none shall see the Lord. In other words, there is a correspondence between the felt realities of a sinful and a regenerate state of the soul; and the pardoned sinner will prize and magnify his Saviour, just in proportion as he has *felt his need* of him.

Miss Bent found that she had much to struggle against, in keeping her covenant vows. She was naturally wild and impulsive; and it was not easy to maintain the meekness and gentleness of Christ; it was not easy to lay aside old habits of feeling and thought and will, and be clothed with humility. Yet she was fully sensible of her peculiar tendencies and trials. "Sister Nancy," she would often say, "can be a Christian with half the effort I can!" Yet she never excused herself for wrong doing on the ground of natural disposition, and early habits. She took blame to herself for whatever in her heart or life, was contrary to the divine requirements, and the spirit of her profession.

As a woman and a Christian, she had marked individuality of character; and was always herself. Perhaps the trait which first impressed an observer, was her independence of character. Her thoughts were her own, and her mode of stating them was her own. She looked upon life from her own point of vision; and adopted purposes and formed plans accordingly. Her views of duty were in accordance with her views of life. Ever faithful to her own settled beliefs, she carried them into practice in her own way. And this independence of thought and opinion, rendered her sometimes liable to be misunderstood; perhaps sometimes appeared, when seen in single acts, like confident forwardness. But actions are to be judged by their motives and circumstances, rather than by comparison; and each man is entitled to his individuality. In Miss Bent's case, there are two facts which are important as throwing light on this matter, and that enable us to draw a right conclusion. 1. She had a sound physical constitution, and uniform good health, which gave her moral life a higher tone and elasticity; and 2. by the loss of her mother in childhood, she was thrown on her own resources, and forced to rely much on herself. Thus robust in health, she did not feel the need of help, as the invalid child does, and could stand the brunt in childhood's battles; and at the facile period when thoughts and feelings and tastes take form, she had not the softening, restraining influence of a mother's love and authority. And being the eldest of the family, she was looked up to, and constantly bore some weight of authority. That these circumstances should give a lasting bias to character, is not surprising.

Another noticeable feature in Miss Bent's character was inherent strength,—the strength which comes of well defined opinions, and a firm purpose. Deep feeling and prompt action are inseparable. Thorough knowledge of one's self and of God, and unfaltering trust in God, are essential to Christian stability. Or to state it more definitely, the strength of the Christian character depends primarily on deep conviction of sin, and unfaltering faith in Christ. Man's moral strength lies in a knowledge of his weakness and a knowledge of his strength. And as his weakness is sin, so his strength is Christ. Hence Paul's paradox,—"When I am weak, then am I strong." And the weakness of sin lies in its guilt, which is seen and felt only through the enlightening and quickening of conscience which is wrought by the Spirit of God. He only who comprehends the nature of this guilt, realizes his desert of the penalty; and he only discerns the full meaning of the cross of Christ, by whom he has redemption. The man's views of Christ then depend on his views of sin; and faith is vital only when conviction is deep. Miss Bent's experiences, while groping her way in darkness to the mercy-seat, will account for the stability of her Christian faith.

She had great force of character. She had the nerve to look calmly at difficulties,—to study their nature, and to weigh their exact power,—and then to turn them aside, or overcome them. Her fearless energy made mountains appear no larger than mole-hills; and what was discouraging to others, was only an exhilarating incitement to her. If an end was good and desirable, there was always, with her, a way to secure it. And she could inspire in others what she felt in herself. In 1806, a dear friend of hers was left a widow in youth, and was sick, a thousand miles away, in what was then the Western wilderness; but she persuaded a brother of this friend to undertake a journey thither, to bring the homesick consumptive back to the parental roof.—No sooner was a class of girls gathered for the beginning of a Sabbath school, than she set to work to gather a class of boys. Indeed she could hardly wait to finish any plan; others could do that; and she must take hold of something new. And perhaps for this reason, she had more to do with the Sabbath school in its earlier years, and less after it had gone into successful operation. And perhaps, with her sanguine temperament, she was over-urgent for results. "The husbandman waiteth for the precious fruit of the earth, and hath long patience for it, until he receive the early and latter rain." She wanted immediate results; to reap the harvest, when the seed was sown. But this made her an efficient member of society, and of the church. There is always need of, and a place for such; as there are always backward and doubting ones enough to clog the wheels, and prevent precipitancy.

Her efficiency as a teacher in the Sabbath school has been indicated by the preceding analysis of her leading characteristics. Thorough in her preparation of the lesson; deeply imbued herself with the spirit of the truths taught; she awakened and concentrated the interest of her class. She was a thorough teacher; and, while under her instruction, her class were thorough scholars. Few have the faculty of gaining and holding the entire attention, and arresting the spirit of childhood at will, and creating more vivid impressions and fixing those impressions permanently, than Miss Bent. Not only the sentiments expressed, but the exact words used in her suggestions and instructions, are securely lodged in the memory of her scholars; and now, after fifty years, are recalled and repeated with pleasure. They are worth remembering, because of their intrinsic value; and for the sake of the Christian motive which prompted them. Her method was direct; her aim single. She would lead the children, in their earliest years, to the Saviour. Said one of her early pupils, on hearing of her death, "I have no doubt that she has gone to heaven, for she has all her lifetime been trying to get others there."

With the stronger elements, and intrepid

courage, she united a sympathy and kindness for the sick and afflicted, which knew no limit. Several instances occurred, where friends or strangers were thrown on her care, away from their home ; and a mother could not have watched over them more tenderly, nor grieved more sincerely when they died.

Miss Bent had large opportunities for observation of life in some of its phases ; and her activity in various religious and educational enterprises, brought her in contact with people of diverse and leading peculiarities and aims. And her habit of estimating things by her own standard, and the decided convictions by which she was guided, naturally led her mind to draw inferences and lessons, which had to her an important value. And in mature life she formed the plan of writing out these incidents and lessons for the benefit of the young. She commenced a series of publications, in the form of narratives and biography, embodying individual and family history, interspersed with moral and religious reflections. She had sent forth "The Happy Merchant," "The Foster Family," "Conrad," and "Edith,"—published by the Massachusetts Sabbath School Society; and left another similar volume ready for the press, and one partly written. These books were well received by the Sabbath schools, for whose libraries they were specially intended. They are all narratives of real life, varied from the actual occurrences only by fictitious names. And they have the attraction which reality always gives to depicted scenes.

As an author, she had skill in representing quiet home life; and in the fidelity to character with which she gave conversations, especially on religious topics. Perhaps she excelled in describing the incidents, and grouping the individuals around the evening fireside, and in the sick-room. Two thoughts were prominent in her mind, and are in a great variety of ways introduced into her pages,—the preciousness of the Bible, and the importance of beginning the life of piety early.

Miss Bent died September 28, 1841, aged fifty-nine years, in the midst of her work and usefulness. She was sick but twelve days. "Her disease was violent, and excruciating beyond conception; but her mind was calm and tranquil. Having placed her hopes in health, and indeed in youth, on the great atoning Sacrifice, she found in the trying hour that she was not deceived. Her confidence in the mediation of Jesus Christ was unusually strong, and her death truly triumphant. Often during the last hours, did she offer the prayer of the dying martyr, 'Lord Jesus, receive my spirit.' Her last words were, 'Tell me, my soul, can this be death?'"

DEACON LUTHER HAVEN.

Deacon Haven was early enlisted in the establishment of a Sabbath school in the Congregational society, and was chosen its first Superintendent. This was due to his energy and practical wisdom, and prominent position in the church and in the community, as well as his devoted piety. Well educated, for the times, always self-possessed, accustomed to public speaking, and well versed in the truths of the Bible, the selection was a fortunate one. He gave an impress and character, and efficient organization to the school, which carried it through its first years, and insured a steady and strong growth. What would have been an experiment with some, was to him, with his clear forecast, and firm will, and fertility of resources, an assured certainty; and with his reverence for the Holy Scriptures, and thorough conscientiousness, and religious principle, the results of his efforts would redound to the glory of God.

Deacon Haven sprung from a Framingham ancestry, though he was born in Holliston. He was brought up after the manner of the Calvinistic system of belief, and morals, in strict integrity, and uprightness, and the fear of the Lord. His mental powers were of a high order; his perceptions quick; his convictions deep; his spirit fervent; his powers of reasoning acute; his conclusions practical and safe.

From his youth up, he was strictly observant of the Sabbath, and constant in attendance on public worship. But he had reached his forty-fourth year, before he entertained the Christian's hope. In 1814, during the revival which had been for some months in progress, while listening to a sermon from the text, "Why stand ye here all the day idle?" the thought came with intense force to his mind, that his own day of life was fast spending, and he was "idle" in God's work; worse than idle in the matter of his soul's salvation; laying up wrath instead of mercy. He felt that this call was *to him;* and he lost no time in speculations, and trial of the expedients which the natural heart suggests, but commenced to seek God at once, and in earnest. If the day was far spent, and the night at hand, so much the more was there need of urgency and diligence. After a season of anxiety, and searching of heart, the blessed Spirit of grace and consolation was revealed to him, and he found peace in believing. He felt the need, and saw clearly the grounds of justification by faith; and built his hope of pardon and full redemption on this sure foundation. "Unto them that believe, he is precious."

With his characteristic determination and force of character, he set about the work of the new life on which he had entered. The doctrines of grace were to him incentives to work out his own salvation with fear and trembling. God working in him to will and to do, was sufficient reason why he should will and do; why he should be wholly subservient to the divine will; why his life should testify of the grace of God. His promptness and faithfulness, and earnest words of exhortation, at the meetings for prayer and conference, were especially prized by his pastor, Dr. Kellogg, and are remembered with special interest by those who were present; remembered because of their peculiar force and appropriateness; and because it had not been customary for laymen to take an active part in such meetings. In some churches, at this period, it was considered out of place for any but the pastor to make an exhortation, or attempt to explain the Scriptures. Indeed in many churches, at this period, conference and prayer meetings were wholly discarded.

At the time of his conversion, so late in life, many habits of mind, and tastes, had become fixed; had become a second nature to him. His style of thought, and ways of expressing thought, could hardly be changed. His knowledge of the world, and quick perception of character, and skill in comparing and weighing ostensible motives and purposes, had given a peculiar pith and point to his methods of expressing himself, and his criticisms of men and manners. He had also naturally a keen appreciation of the ludicrous in human conduct and thought, and was remarkably quick and felicitous at repartee. His generous heart prompted a sparing use of these powers, but he sometimes wounded deeply by his incisive thrusts. He abhorred all pretense and dissembling, and loved truth and sincerity; paid homage to pure motives and sterling integrity.

That after forty years, customary views and methods, and leading traits and habits should retain their vitality, and turn the thoughts and feelings in the old channels, is not strange. And that they should sometimes cast reproach on " the new man which after God is created in righteousness and true holiness," is accordant with human experience. He did not feel called upon to repress all these habitual impulses, and cut his style of expression to anybody's pattern; he believed that their indulgence within proper limits, is innocent, and conducive to one's own and others' happiness; but he felt the need of watchfulness, and often had to regret a stinging answer which unconsciously escaped him. And he always had more edge than polish; more of the outspoken bluntness, and less of the gentleness of Christ.

But his godly sincerity none doubted. And where grave and serious concerns were at issue, he saw nothing but the weighty reality; where wise counsels were necessary, he could concentrate all his powers; where words were deeds, his words were well chosen. In anxious deliberations for the well-being of the church, and in carrying out measures for the extension of pure and undefiled religion, his heart and mind were enlisted, and he was governed by the spirit of his divine Master. Moral obligation to God was a first motive in his plans, and directed his moral acts. If duty to God was plain, no other questions required his thoughts. He ever had a deep sense of God's goodness and long-suffering, in sparing him, and waiting on him to be gracious, while he was serving sin. And his sense of the condescension of the Son of God in giving his life a ransom, was sometimes almost overpowering. His voice would become tremulous from emotion, as he gave utterance in prayer and exhortation, to his experiences of loving-kindness, and his views of the merciful dispensation, which received its finished efficacy at the cross on Calvary.

When in 1816, the plan of opening a Sabbath school was suggested, Deacon Haven was found ready for the work. As the method and its details were yet to be settled, there was need of forecast and constructive ability, as well as zeal and hopefulness. He had habits of careful observation, and a reflective mind, and the calmness to look on all sides of a new subject, before adopting a conclusion. He had the good common sense that can see what is to be done, and how best to do it. And what was peculiarly necessary, he had the insight into character which enabled him to judge what part each person associated with him could be relied on to do ; to judge if the zeal of one would hold out, and the doubts of another would be convinced, and how the various opinions could be harmonized. Without apparent effort, he would contrive to make the most of individuals; to give them the place they could fill with best acceptance and advantage. And having broad and generous aims, and a heart consecrated to the cause, his plans and management as Superintendent, at this critical period, proved eminently wise. Literally, he laid "the foundations of many generations."

Perhaps the traits by which Deacon Haven was most distinguished, were, the clearness and precision of his views, and his unswerving obedience to duty. His standard of Christian character was well-defined, and elevated; and he tried himself and others by it; and condemned, as heartily in himself as in others, neglects and deficiencies. The doctrines of the gospel, as they presented themselves to his mind for belief, took a definite form, and arranged themselves in a harmonious system. He was accustomed to study the Bible for himself, and knew its own grounds of truth, and could give a reason of the hope that was in him. Through all his Christian life, he "held fast the form of sound words, in faith and love which is in Christ Jesus."

And in action, convictions of right and duty impelled and guided, and not the impulse of mere feeling. This gave him his peculiar power; gave him the elements of a positive rather than a negative life; gave him the force of character, which makes its own way, and leaves its own impression on society.

And the fact that he had decided and well defined views, and yielded implicit obedience to the right, to the dictates of his own conscience, sometimes brought him into antagonism with others; with friends as well as foes. This always lays a man open to misconstruction and unjust criticism. It is so common to study the *policy* of plans and actions, that the bold pursuit of right is not appreciated; indeed, is not understood. The strait and narrow way which Christ trod, and which leadeth unto life will always have few travellers, and they will be "set at nought" as their leader was, and will have little influence in the great world of business, and distinction, and earthly reward.

With more of the impulsive element in his character, and more of pliability, his popularity would have been greater—perhaps his influence not more salutary. He whose life attracts notice, and who makes an *immediate* impression on society, is he who has quick sensibility, and obeys the impulse of the moment. He goes with a rush—like the mountain torrent from melting snows; but his power ceases with his popularity, or his active life. The man who makes the deepest and a lasting impression on society, must have quick sensibility, but a quicker conscience; must be capable of being deeply stirred and thoroughly aroused, but through appeals to his judgment—through the apprehension of the understanding; and must act with energy and courage, but without nervous excitement and transient emotion. To flash forth like the meteor or lightning, may only produce disturbance, perhaps destruction; it is the steady light of the sun that warms and invigorates, and brings the fruits to perfection.

Deacon Haven retained his interest in the Sabbath school, and was ever active in various ways in its support; and after a retirement of eleven years was called a second time to the superintendency.

He loved the church, and sought its purity and enlargement; loved and cherished it in prosperity and in perils; stood by its doctrines and discipline; to the last "holding the Head," and believing that "other foundation can no man lay than that is laid, which is Jesus Christ."

He died July 11, 1851, at the advanced age of eighty-one. "The righteous shall be in everlasting remembrance."

MARY BROWN. (Mrs. Jonas Colburn.)

Miss Brown was a native of this town, and was educated at the Framingham Academy and at Mr. Emerson's school in Byfield. Though her father resided three miles from the centre village, she boarded at home while attending school, and was noted for her punctuality and thorough scholarship.

After completing a course of English studies at the academy, she went in 1812 to Canada, where she spent four years in teaching. She afterwards taught school in her own district in Framingham, and in neighboring towns.

She was the subject of special religious convictions, and dated her hope of a gracious change in the year 1813, when 22 years old.

She was married to Rev. Jonas Colburn in 1823, passing the next twenty years of her life at Leverett and Stoneham, in this State, and at Wells, Maine.

Miss Brown was in Framingham in the autumn of 1816, and was present at the first consultation in reference to opening a Sabbath school, in which she felt a deep interest, and readily undertook her share of the labor. She was constantly present, and took part in teaching the first class of girls gathered, and had charge of a class till her marriage in 1823, except when absent teaching, or at school in Byfield.

Her qualifications for instruction were superior, both of mind and character. With good culture and a well-stored memory, she had a remarkable faculty of attaching children to her and gaining their good will. Possessing a genial, sympathetic nature, and a kind of intuitive perception of the most direct way to a child's heart, she could inspire courage in the timid, and help the hesitating over the stumbling-blocks with so little seeming effort that they scarcely knew they were helped, and were surprised to find themselves reciting so acceptably. She would succeed in establishing a perfect understanding and acquaintance with her class, in a brief time, and having won their confidence would lead them along at her will. She was equally at home with the little ones of six, and the lads and misses of sixteen; and was equally successful in imparting instruction, and acquiring a moral ascendency.

And this interest in the young, and power to win their confidence, and to impress her own thoughts upon their minds, continued through life. One who knew her first when over fifty years old, says, " My earliest recollections of

Mrs. Colburn are of her sweet smile and winning ways, as when quite a child I used to visit at her house. I think I must have been about seven years old. Even then, I remember, she often spoke to me of the love of Jesus in such gentle tones as touched my childish heart, and made an ineffaceable impression."

She knew her peculiar gift; she felt that this was a "talent" intrusted to her, and sought to make it yield large gain to her Lord. Hence this power was, after her conversion, held subservient to, and directed by love to her Savior. She endeavored to take advantage of the confidence bestowed on her, to lead the children to the truth, and to Him who is the Way and the Truth and the Life.

Seen then with her natural endowments of mind and heart; or seen when to these were added the graces of the Spirit, "everybody loved her." To children and their parents, to old and young alike, her presence was an inspiration and a joy.

Miss Brown had naturally a high flow of spirits, and great conversational powers. She had ready humor, a playful fancy, a keen appreciation of the beautiful, and a quick sympathy, which, added to enough of confidence in herself to make her master of her thoughts and words, rendered her a most entertaining talker. She would catch the spirit of the time and place, and take the lead, or bear her part with equal felicity. She had read much, and remembered vividly the facts and incidents, and could recall them when she wanted them for use.

She had peculiar elasticity of mind. Her thoughts would bound off from point to point, like the antelope over the rocks and hills. And yet it was not at random. She seemed to have her fancy, and her memory, and her reasoning powers, all in harness, and in hand, and to press them to the race for the very joy of it. Her own spirit received pleasure, while she imparted pleasure to her friends.

This habit of entertaining her friends by her conversational powers, in which she indulged without restraint in youth, caused her much anxiety in maturer life. She felt that her usefulness and happiness would be promoted, by maintaining her youthful vivacity and sympathy. The love for the beautiful, and the relish of mental excitement, when mind meets mind, and heart comes in contact with heart, and the bright scintillations of thought and feeling are evolved, were inwrought in her nature so deeply, that to fetter her emotions and limit their expression in words, was like obstructing the life current. But to decide how far Christian principle should restrain and modify her ruling passion; to fix the dividing line between safety and danger, was not easy. It cost her many struggles and fears. And her closet could probably testify to many an hour of regrets and tears, consequent upon an evening spent in social enjoyment, where she gave way to the old time levity.

That reserve and a clouded brow are no part of religion, is plain. That a cheerful spirit, and the highest culture of the social nature, is consistent with piety, is plain. That to be happy and to make others happy, is a part of religion, is equally plain. That to keep one's self young in impulses and feelings and hopes, is promotive of one's influence over the young, is unquestioned. That good sense, and quick intelligence, and warm emotions, and a fit method of expressing them, are parts of the "talent" intrusted to the Christian, is unquestionable. But precisely where is the line between innocent mirth, and hurtful levity; wherein reverence for God should restrain our natural impulses; how far the great realities of moral obligation and immortality—of sin and holiness—consist with social amusements, and the trivial obligations of this fleeting life; at what point devotion to friends interferes with devotion to God;—may well cause the conscientious Christian anxious inquiry.

And then the power of example, and the risk that our example may be an "offence" to any; and that it may be misjudged, and give occasion for false inferences in regard to ourselves, and be made a justification for unrestrained license of frivolity and worldly-mindedness in others, is a sufficient reason why we should "keep the door of our lips." Christians are not always aware how closely they are watched, even by those who have no doubt of their Christian character; not so much, perhaps, from a curiosity to see how a Christian acts, as from a conviction that a Christian has no right to forget, even for a moment, his religious obligations.

Later in life, Mrs. Colburn showed in a marked degree, the chastening effect of affliction, and the sadder realities of life. For there is a shady side, as well as a cloud with a silver lining, in the experience of most pastors' wives, —of most of Christ's chosen ones; tests of one or another natural or gracious affection; that the beauty of holiness may appear in His true children. She could readily make and attach to herself new friends; but her best social delights were in old friends,—her heart *rested in* the confidence and communion of tried and congenial love. One of her peculiar trials was the breaking up of friendships attendant on removals from one parish to another. It was a strain on her sensitive nature, which colder hearts cannot understand. But sorest of all was the death of her two dearly loved daughters, in their early infancy; just when the wealth of a mother's tenderness and affection is poured out most freely, and the first artless tokens of love returned, are revealed to a mother's eye.

But the trial was a fire that purifies. There was manifest a deeper spirituality; and unfailing faith in that precious love of the Saviour towards her, which was the spring of her life, supported her. And as her nature recovered itself, a new and unwonted strength was apparent; a firmer hold on the divine promises; a clearer insight into the divine mercy; a sweet and loving nearness to him who took her little ones; a yearning, not to recall them, but to meet them in his bosom. The old bounding elasticity of spirits remained, as an essential part of herself; but chastened, refined, consecrated. The playfulness of fancy, and thorough sympathy with the hearty mirth of childhood remained; but it was easier for her to fix the limit to her feelings and words.

There is a mourning, that "will not be comforted,"—that buries itself in the grave with the loved and lost; a grief, which faints under rebukes,—which weakens and wastes, and brings a premature oldness. And there is a cherishing the memory of departed ones, especially of beloved children; a keeping fresh the feelings that centred in their life, and awakened our hopes in them, *that keeps our hearts as young as when they died.* Henceforth they are to us just what they were then; and we think of them and ourselves as living together in the charmed and changeless oasis; the spring-time has no summer; the fragrant morning has no hot noon; the opening rose remains a bud. And this consecration of affection,—of the entwined ties of life; this baptism into a new experience, where our Heavenly Father took his own, and left us his blessing,—tracing with his own finger on the rainbow of promise which spanned the dark cloud, his name and pledge, *Jehovah-jireh,*—gives a tone and coloring to our life and character; is—to the true Christian— the sanctification which cometh of God.

From this time forth, her interest in children had a new element, and a new aim. The thought, thus made a reality to her, that they may be early called, inspired her to be faithful in efforts to instruct them in the Bible, and to win them to Christ.

Among the influences which gave a distinctive bent, and its completeness to the character of Mrs. Colburn, and developed her tastes, and habits of thought, none was so important as the Bible.

She heard it read by her father in his family, who was very careful to enjoin a silent and respectful attention; and at the age of five years, she commenced reading it in course. And this custom she continued through life. Probably not a day passed—except in severe sickness—for sixty-two years, in which she did not read from one to five chapters.

In early youth she was attracted by its histories and biographies; and its rich imagery, and sweet and sublime poetry, found answering harmonies in her keen sensibility, and refined mind. After she had tasted that the Lord is gracious, and had drunk at the living fountain, she read the Bible for its own sake, and its Author's sake. She loved the inspired and inspiring truths,—the doctrines, the promises, the plan of salvation, the immortality brought to light, the revealed realities of this life and the life to come,—" more to be desired than gold, yea, than much fine gold; sweeter also than honey and the honeycomb."

So truly did she appreciate the Holy Book, so filled was her mind with its truths and facts, so fully in sympathy was her heart with its spirit and power, that she seemed unconsciously *to think in its language and images.*

In conversation with friends and strangers, on the common incidents and plans of life, as well as on religious themes, a Scripture expression, as the medium of her thought, came as naturally as her breathing. Her letters, which her friends were wont to prize for their treasures of affection, and kind interest, and fitness of thought, abounded in allusions and quotations from God's Word.

Says one of her most intimate friends, " The Bible was her study and delight, and nothing relieved weariness and alleviated sorrow like a perusal of its pages." So familiar was she with every part of the sacred volume, that when any one read a chapter, she could prompt, or correct, or go on if they stopped.

And she was well versed in the Assembly's Shorter Catechism. She had learned it perfectly in childhood, and through life was accustomed to repeat it—the whole catechism—to herself every Saturday evening. This exercise and her usual chapter in the Bible would bring her feelings in unison with the holy rest of the Sabbath. This little compendium of truth probably expressed very nearly her religious creed, as a clear statement of what the Scriptures teach in regard to man's nature and relations to God, and the plan of salvation.

It scarcely need be said, that a character formed under the united influence and inspiration of the Bible and Catechism, will possess symmetry and strength, will have the elements of a vigorous activity, and well-adjusted proportions. There will be motive to arouse the mental and moral faculties; there will be ends to gain, personal and social, high and noble; there are means supplied suited to strong and enduring effort. With the grace of Christ in the soul, and the glory of Christ to live for, and following the light of the blessed Word—which shines in the heart as well as forward on the path—no power will be idle; every power will find its best development; every power will be in harmony with a regenerate life; all the powers will work together for good.

Her naturally quick perception and self-possession, were of great advantage in the conscientious and faithful discharge of duty. Her Christian thought and action had fitness, as well as force and beauty. Having a zeal of God, but not according to knowledge, is a weakness, even in the sincere Christian; and his tongue often nullifies the power of his godly life, which by itself would have a sweet savor of Christ.

And her superior endowments of mind fitted her to exert an influence on the educated. Perhaps few of her sex have had more success in presenting truth to, and awakening the conscience of students and men of thought. She readily grasped principles and deeper relations, and easily followed logical reasoning. She had a relish for investigation, particularly in theological studies, and was familiar with the grounds and bearings of moral and religious truth. But she was most at home in the thoughts and truths of the Bible; these were in her heart and memory, and she could use them with great skill. And in her mouth, the texts of Scripture were not suggestive of controversy, but of personal concern and belief—"a discerner of the thoughts and intents of the heart." Quickening and imparting strength to her own soul, they spoke with vital force to the souls of others. Thus could she influence the will and heart, and lead to duty. Thus her daily practice and daily delight were, to bear witness to the truth, and recommend the Son of God and His religion to all with whom she was in any degree conversant.

She did not wait for duty to come in her way; she sought it out, made inquiry of God and of conscience for something to do which should promote the welfare of souls. It was not enough for her to lead those who were seeking Him, to the Saviour; but she went to those who were standing afar off, and by all her persuasive influence endeavored to win them to faith and love. This was her idea of Christian obligation, and the prompting of her heart. And to such there is always enough to do, and wisdom to do it, and "the joy of the Lord is their strength."

Herein is the secret of a successful, happy, Christian life. To wait on the Lord, as they that watch for the morning, is to find Him a present help. To take up the cross and follow Christ, is to discover his sufficiency and infinite worthiness, and to have his joy fulfilled in themselves, and to find rest to their souls.

Religion brought forth largely in her its gentle and characteristic fruits,—a childlike trust and assurance, and that nearness to God which finds its best expression in prayer. Like her of Bethany, she loved to sit at the feet of Jesus, and hear his words. And every word which he spoke was believed and cherished. To her, faith was trust as well as belief; was that insight and assurance which participates in the life of Christ; which daily partakes of the heavenly manna; which makes the joy and purity of the future, present realities to the soul.

She loved the sanctuary, as the place of worship, and she loved the retirement of her closet, as the place of communion with her Saviour. She learned an important lesson on the value of prayer in early life. Having opened a school in the village of W. she found her resources taxed, and her patience tried by a number of turbulent spirits, and was almost ready to give up in discouragement. Meeting Mrs. S., a trusted friend, she said, " I'm discouraged! Those large rough boys don't respect me, and I cannot manage them!"

" Pray in your school, and they'll respect you."

" Oh, I cannot!"

" Try it, and see. Grace comes in the way of duty when we need it."

On reflection she determined to try. She opened the morning sessions of the school with prayer; and from that time, to her surprise and joy, found that even the roughest were respectful, and her authority was established.

An experience of this kind could not but have a deep significance to one as observant of the ways of God and man as was Miss Brown. She was led into a great mystery, without seeing the hand that opened the door; and found it all light and well adjusted within; found that the divine purposes and prayer were not antagonistic; found that prayer was God's medium of working out some of his purposes, and blessing the soul that prays. She had no occasion to look on the doctrinal side of this duty. She had the "faith which works by love;" she found delight in holy communion; she found strength in waiting on God; she found "the secret of the Lord was with them that fear him, and that he will show them his covenant."

With maturer views and experiences of the the Christian life, prayer became a vital element of her piety; and it was the way in which she obtained spiritual blessings for herself and others. As the dutiful child goes to its father for proper favors, so she went to God—not

alone in difficulty and danger, but always—
whenever affection and reverence, as well as
need prompted. The promise, "Ask, and ye
shall receive," had to her the same force as all
the Master's teachings. And in her own
spiritual needs she went to Him who could
help ; in the spiritual needs of her friends,
she carried them to Him who could help.
When she had urged personal duty and immediate
attention to religion on one brought
within her influence, she would carry the case
to God, and thenceforth fidelity and prayer
were co-operative, till the individual found pardon
at the cross, or passed beyond her reach.

Rev. Dr. Hitchcock, pastor of the College
Church where she attended, in his address at
her funeral, remarked that " he knew no person
who had done more for Amherst College, by
her prayers and efforts to bring young men to
Christ."

After leaving the settled pastoral life, Mr. and
Mrs. Colburn removed to Amherst, where she
passed seven or eight years, in duties as she
had opportunity, and enjoying the literary and
religious advantages of the place, and the
society of old friends and new. They were
active and blessed years to her.

They then spent three years in Framingham, on the "old homestead" where Mrs. Colburn was born, and spent her childhood. But it was not the *old home*. Thirty-five years had wrought great changes. A generation had passed away. Except her brother and a few scattered families, all were strangers. The Academy, and Town House, and Meeting-House were gone. The old trees by the roadside, under whose shade she had rested on the way to school and to church, were cut down, and the young ones in their stead had no grateful associations and memories.

Besides, the location was not convenient to religious and other privileges, which were to her, "more than her necessary food." And her failing health admonished her that it was time to find a quiet retreat, and "set her house in order."

Her parting with the scene of her childhood —as she realized it, a final parting—was characteristic. Says her sister: "It was arranged that she should spend the last night at our house, and leave us in the morning direct for the cars. Mary came in the afternoon, and staid to tea. She was cheerful and happy, and quite herself, and said nothing of any change of plan for the night. Just at sunset, I noticed her standing at that east window looking intently out, (the window commanded a full view of the old home farm,) *silent*. I said, 'Mary, what are you doing?'"

"'Taking my leave of my early home, and of you all!'

"After looking long, she turned, saying, 'I had better pass the night at the old place, and leave from there in the morning. It will be as much as I can bear. I shan't see you in the morning. I have you all in my heart!'" And with a kiss, she left her brother's hospitable roof and kind family.

There is deep meaning, and moral beauty in this *silent leave-taking*. Looking out at that window, with all the faculties gathered up, and the inner consciousness and reflective powers concentrated, was living over again the past; was fixing the memories of that past and the impressions of the present in one group; and associating the love of friends with the scenes and proofs of that love.

This was Mrs. Colburn's only leave-taking. She died alone, and was spared all the pangs of parting with friends.

After an absence of five years, they returned to Amherst, in the spring of 1857, to occupy a house just purchased by Mr. C.; and from this time till the opening of summer, were busy in fitting it up, and gathering those conveniences and comforts and simple luxuries they had need of. Here they had fixed their earthly home; and in the immediate neighborhood of a few choice friends, and amid the refined society, and pleasant associations of the village, they expected to pass the evening of life.

Mrs. Colburn was sensible that her active work was done; and that her health was gradually declining. She had some premonitory symptoms of heart disease, whose liabilities she well understood. But she had need to make no special change in her plans, and no cause for new solicitude. *Heaven was near;* and Christ had tasted death for her.

During July, Mr. Colburn was supplying a vacant pulpit in Connecticut, which rendered it desirable for him to be absent through the week. At his urgent request, she consented that a young lady friend should come in and pass the nights with her; "Not," as she said, "because I am lonely; for my Saviour is always present with me, and I am not afraid."

One very warm afternoon she was out making calls on a few particular friends. Nothing unusual was noticed in the state of her health, further than the effect of the extreme heat.

Her spirits were buoyant, and her conversation sparkling,—full of pleasant fancies, and happy turns of thought, and rich in spirituality. Her cup of happiness seemed to be full, and running over. When about leaving the door of Mrs. M., with whom her relations had been most intimate, she said, with a half playful smile, "Before you know it, I shall fly away,"—alluding evidently to the Psalmist's wish,—"O that I had wings like a dove, for then would I fly away, and be at rest." She knew not that it was prophetic, and that the prophecy was so near its fulfilment.

The last call made before reaching her own house, was protracted for an hour. She felt specially at home in this family, because of some early associations, and a similarity of present condition. One of the daughters was her companion, during the absence of her husband. The presence of these girls, and her desire to do them good, carried her mind back to her own childhood. She recalled its bright pictures of gayety and frolic, which were shaded by the reflection that those first years, which were offered so willingly to the world, belonged to God. She spoke of her happy school days; of the living and the dead,—passing with easy transition from gay to grave. But her mind dwelt with special pleasure on the kind providence of God, which in a number of instances, had kept her when in danger; and on the sovereign grace of God by which he had adopted her as his child. Referring to the present, she said: "I don't expect to live a great while. No one enjoys life better than I do. I am settled where I have long desired to pass a few pleasant, quiet years. I like our new place, and have just got the house fitted up to my taste. I feel that I could enjoy many years in it. But I hardly expect it." So was she partaking of the delights of Christian friendship, and so was she resting in God, with the sweet assurance which says, Thy will be done!

"Early in the evening," says her young friend, "when I went to her house, I found Mrs. C. seated in the door-way, listening to music in the house opposite. She seemed rested, and gave me her usual cordial reception, and we soon went into the sitting-room. Her conversation this evening, was mainly on religious subjects; much of it relating to her own experience and hopes. Among other things, she said: 'I am now in my sixty-seventh year, and I have read the Bible through sixty-nine times—twice with Scott's Notes—and am partly through the seventieth time.'

At bedtime, as was our custom, I read a chapter from the Bible, and she offered prayer. The prayer I can never forget. The sweet, loving spirit which pervaded her whole life was evinced in her petitions, and expressions of gratitude and trust. It seemed as if she was standing on the threshold of heaven, talking with her Saviour, so simple, and yet so earnest was her pleading for herself and for others.

Bidding her good night, I went up stairs, as she preferred sleeping alone. In the morning she rose about six and called me, saying, "Do not hasten, Mary, if you are tired; but I knew you wanted to finish your dress, and so called you." As usual, she laid down again after calling me. Going down stairs, I looked into her room, to bid her good morning, but found her sleeping quietly, her breathing as regular as a child's.

At noon, Mrs. M. sent in a choice piece of her own prepared dinner, thinking that Mrs. Colburn might relish it. But the little girl found her dead!"

It seems that she had risen, and partly dressed; and perhaps feeling faint, had laid down, and died. There had evidently been no struggle, and no suffering. Her countenance wore a sweet smile, as if she had heard the

Saviour's voice calling, "Come up higher!" and in the first joy of the summons, had sped away. "Blessed are the dead which die in the Lord from henceforth; yea, saith the Spirit, that they may rest from their labors; and their works do follow them."

SKETCH OF THE RISE OF SABBATH SCHOOLS.

[In most cases, pertaining to our own country, the facts here given are taken from official statements published at the time, by pastors and superintendents.]

1781. The first general system of Sunday schools in England, grew out of the efforts of Robert Raikes. In 1781, he established schools in his native town of Gloucester; and in a short time they were extended to the principal cities and towns.

The occasion, as well as the primary design of these schools, are clearly set forth in the following letter from Mr. Raikes to Colonel Townley:—

"The beginning of this scheme was entirely owing to accident. Some business leading me, one morning, into the suburbs of the city, where the lowest of the people chiefly reside, I was struck with concern at seeing a group of children, wretchedly ragged, at play in the street. I asked an inhabitant whether those children belonged to that part of the town, and lamented their misery and idleness. 'Ah!

sir,' said the woman, 'could you take a view of this part of the town on a Sunday, you would be shocked indeed; for then the street is filled with multitudes of these wretches, who, released on that day from employment, spend their time in noise and riot, playing at chuck, and cursing and swearing in a manner so horrid, as to convey to any serious mind an idea of hell rather than any other place.'

"This conversation suggested to me that it would be at least a harmless attempt, if it were productive of no good, should some little plan be formed to check this deplorable profanation of the Sabbath. I then inquired of the woman if there were any decent, well-disposed women in the neighborhood, who kept schools for teaching to read. I presently was directed to four. To them I applied, and made an agreement with them to receive as many children as I should send upon a Sunday, whom they were to instruct in reading and in the Church Catechism. For this, I engaged to pay them each a shilling for their day's employment.

"I then waited on the clergyman, and imparted to him my plan. He was so much satisfied with the idea, that he engaged to lend his assistance, by going round to the schools on a Sunday afternoon, to examine the progress

RISE OF SABBATH SCHOOLS. 133

that was made, and to enforce order and decorum among such a set of little heathens.

"This was the commencement of the plan. It is now about three years since we began, and I wish you were here to make inquiry into the effect. A woman, who lives in a lane where I had fixed a school, told me, some time ago, that the place was quite a heaven upon Sundays compared with what it used to be. The numbers who have learned to read and say their catechism are so great, that I am quite astonished at it. Upon the Sunday afternoon the mistresses take their scholars to church, a place into which neither they nor their ancestors ever entered, with a view to the glory of God. But, what is yet more extraordinary, within this month these little ragamuffins have in great numbers taken it into their heads to frequent the early morning prayers, which are held every morning at the cathedral at seven o'clock. I believe there were near fifty this morning. They assemble at the house of one of the mistresses, and walk before her to church, two and two, in as much order as a company of soldiers. I am generally at church, and after service they all come round me to make their bows, and, if any animosities have arisen, to make their complaint. The great principle I inculcate is, to be kind and good-natured to each other ; not to provoke one another ; to be dutiful to their parents ; not to offend God by cursing or swearing ; and such little plain precepts as all may comprehend. The success that has attended this scheme has induced one or two of my friends to adopt the plan, and set up Sunday schools in other parts of the city; and now a whole parish has taken up the object, so that I flatter myself, in time the good effects will appear so conspicuous as to become generally adopted. The number of children at present thus engaged on the Sabbath is between two and three hundred, and they are increasing every week, as the benefit is universally seen. I have endeavored to engage the clergy of my acquaintance that reside in their parishes. One has entered into the scheme with great fervor.

"I cannot express to you the pleasure I often receive in discovering genius and innate good dispositions among this little multitude. It is botanizing in human nature. I have often, too, the satisfaction of receiving thanks from parents, for the reformation they perceive in their children. Often have I given them kind admonitions, which I always do in the mildest and gentlest manner. The going among them, doing them little kindnesses, distributing trifling rewards, and ingratiating myself with them, I hear, have given me an ascendency greater than I ever could have imagined; for I am told by their mistresses that they are very much afraid of my displeasure. If you ever pass through Gloucester, I shall be happy to pay my respects to you, and to show you the effects of this effort at civilization. If the glory of God be promoted in any, even the smallest degree, society must reap some benefit. If good seed be sown in the mind at an early period of human life, though it shows not itself again for many years, it may please God, at some future period, to cause it to spring up, and bring forth a plenteous harvest.

"With regard to the rules adopted, I only require that they come to the school on Sunday as clean as possible. Many were at first deterred because they wanted decent clothing; but I could not undertake to supply this defect. I argue, therefore, if you can loiter about without shoes and in a ragged coat, you may as well come to school and learn what may tend to your good, in that garb. I reject none on that footing. All that I require, are clean hands, clean face, and the hair combed; if you have no clean shirt, come in what you have on.

The want of decent apparel, at first, kept great numbers at a distance; but they now begin to grow wiser, and are all pressing to learn. I have had the good luck to procure places for some that were deserving, which has been of great use.

"You will understand that these children are from six years old to twelve or fourteen. Boys and girls above this age, who have been totally undisciplined, are generally too refractory for this government. A reformation in society seems to me only practicable by establishing motives of duty, and practical habits of order and decorum, at an early age. But whither am I running? I am ashamed to see how much I have trespassed on your patience; but I thought the most complete idea of Sunday schools was to be conveyed to you by telling what first suggested the thought."

1782. Sabbath schools were established in Scotland as early as 1782. As provision was made for primary instruction for all classes, the schools there were of strictly a religious character. "Scotland, has the honor, therefore, of instituting the first Sabbath schools in Protestant countries, for the purpose solely of religious instruction."

1791. Sabbath schools, after the plan of Mr. Raikes, were first formed in Philadelphia, in 1791.

1794. A Sunday school was started in Paterson, N. J., in 1794, by Sarah Colt, a little girl eleven years of age. She collected the children of the factories together, and taught them from Sunday to Sunday, until she had as many as sixty under her care. She was a teacher for forty years.

1797. In 1797, a Sunday school, on the same system, was established at Pawtucket, R. I. It was commenced at the suggestion of Samuel Slater, Esq., by Mr. Collier, a student in Brown University.

This, and all the first Sabbath schools gathered in New England, were individual enterprises. Those in the country towns were for moral and religious instruction; those in the city, and seaboard towns, were patterned somewhat after the English system.

That there should be need to teach the children of any class of our citizens in Massachusetts, the elements of education, in Sunday, or charity schools, may seem strange to us, who are wont to suppose that the system of free schools was coeval with the establishment of civil society. But as late as 1817, in Boston, says a well-informed writer, "Children are not admitted into our town schools under seven years of age, and not even then, unless they can read without spelling, and well enough to be classed; by which regulation children of those parents too poor to pay for private instruction, are inevitably cut off from that education which *in appearance* is open to all. Hence, the necessity of charity schools. And in every view, the Sunday school, for combined instruction in reading and religion most directly and effectually meets the want here described."

1805. The first Sabbath school in New England, for the sole purpose of the religious instruction of children, so far as is now known, was established in Bath, N. H., in 1805. Shortly before, the Rev. David Sutherland (who had been engaged in early efforts to found Sabbath schools in Scotland, his native country,) was settled as pastor of the church in Bath, and at once started a Sabbath school in the principal village, which he conducted with various success, and with very little aid from others, for thirteen years. In 1817, a new spirit was awakened, and other schools were opened in different parts of the town.

1810. In 1810, Sabbath schools began to be established in Massachusetts. In that year, two schools were formed,—one in Concord and one in Beverly.

1810. The school in Concord was opened by a young lady, Miss Sarah Ripley, daughter of Rev. Dr. Ripley. She gathered a few children upon Sabbath afternoons after church, at her father's house, and taught them the Scriptures and catechism. After this school had continued four or five years, through the warm season, three pious young ladies opened a Sabbath school in a room at the house now (1868) occupied by Mrs. Charles Davis, in the centre of the town. But the people generally did not give their influence to the project; and a regular Sabbath school was not organized till June, 1818; when a school of one hundred and thirty pupils, and eleven teachers, four males and seven females, was started. The grammar school-master was Superintendent.

1810. The school in Beverly was commenced by two young ladies, Joanna Prince and Hannah Hill. Miss Prince was teaching a day school in a room of her mother's house. She and Miss Hill opened a Sabbath school in her school room. This school was held in the morning, and after the afternoon service. About thirty scholars attended the first season. Some of the members were very zealous in learning to read, while others had long Scripture lessons to recite from memory. The ladies continued their school, all by themselves, with great success, for three years. After the third year the enterprise was taken up by others, and a general school was established, in which all the societies united. Soon, however, separate parish schools were established.

1812. " The first Sabbath school in Boston was established, by a lady, in 1812. While on a visit to Beverly, in October of that year, she heard of the school in that place, and although she did not see it, she was at once impressed with the importance of a similar one in Boston, and on her return immediately commenced the work.. This school was continued until the year 1822.

" Charles Walley, Esq., having heard of the enterprise of this lady, sent her a donation of books for her school, consisting of six Bibles, twelve New Testaments, twelve Watts' Shorter Catechisms, twelve Watts' Divine Songs for Children, and twelve Hymns for Infant Minds, —in all fifty-four volumes. This donation constituted the *first Sabbath school library* in Boston."

1812. In 1812, a Sunday school was commenced in Brunswick, Me.

1813. "In the winter of 1812–13, a Sabbath school was formed in Salem, under the patronage of a company of ladies belonging to the society of the Rev. Dr. Hopkins. The pupils were placed under the tuition of a teacher of a school of young ladies."

1813. In the course of the same year, 1813, a school was opened at the Tabernacle church in Salem. It was kept for one hour before the afternoon service. Except one summer, it was continued for five years, the number of teachers varying from ten to twenty, and the scholars from one hundred to two hundred.

1814. A Sabbath school was established in Newburyport, in 1814, by Miss E. E. Carter, and three other young ladies. As a preliminary step, one of them went to Dr. Samuel Spring, and requested the use of his vestry. The Doctor replied that he himself would have no objection to the establishment of such a school; but he feared some of his good people might think it to be too secular an employment for the Sabbath. They however ventured to occupy the vestry, and without aid or co-operation from the church, began their benevolent undertaking. The first year, the number was about one hundred. The school began after public service in the afternoon, and occupied more than three hours. In 1815, the school was intrusted to some members of Dr. Spring's society, and two of the ladies commenced another in a more destitute part of the town. In the summer of this year, 1815, Miss Carter started a Sabbath school at Kennebunkport, Me.

1814. In June, 1814, two ladies of New York opened in that city a Sabbath school for adults and children, in which were collected eighty or ninety pupils.

1814. In the same year, 1814, a Sabbath school was established in Wilmington, Del.

1814. In the autumn of 1814, a school was established at Cambridgeport, in connection with Rev. Thomas B. Gannett's society.

1815. In 1815, the Salem Street or Christ Church Sunday school in Boston was instituted. This school attracted much public notice, and was for a time supposed to be the first school for religious instruction formed in the State. In six months from its commencement, the pupils numbered two hundred and fifty. It continued to prosper for many years under the superintendency of Mr. J. W. Ingraham.

1815. In the same year, 1815, Sabbath schools were commenced in the Northern Liberties of Philadelphia, which in a few months contained no less than five hundred pupils. In 1816 they were generally introduced, and connected with most of the parishes in that city.

1815. In May, 1815, Sunday schools were formed in Newark, N. J. During the first summer the number of pupils gradually increased to four hundred and forty, comprising all classes, rich and poor. In 1816 the schools were confined to the poor.

1816. A Sunday school was instituted in Chillicothe, Ohio, in April, 1816, by two young men, who agreed to bear equally the expense. At first it was kept in a private room. In four weeks it had so increased, that it was removed to a large room in the upper story of the Academy, and the list of pupils was swelled to one hundred.

1816. In the spring of 1816, a few pious females, desirous of promoting the religious welfare of children, opened a Sabbath school in Westborough, and continued it through two seasons. In 1818 a society was formed, and a large school organized. The young ladies to whom the honor of this movement belongs were Arethusa Brigham, Hannah Fay, Abagail Gregory, Maria Brigham, and the two Misses Bates.

1816. A Sabbath school for the religious instruction of children was opened in Cambridge in 1816. Until 1818 it was small, and limited in influence. Then several young ladies offered their services as teachers, and a young man took charge of the older boys, and superintended the school. A large number were gathered in, and the school was very prosperous.

1816. The first Sabbath school was opened in Providence, R. I., in 1816.

1816. A biblical and catechetical school was instituted at Greensborough and Hardwick, Vt., June 25, 1816. The number of children under instruction the first year was three hundred.

1816. A Sabbath school was opened in Carlisle, Penn., early in the summer of 1816.

1816. In June 1816, the females of the Third Baptist Church in Boston (Dr. Sharp's,) formed a Sabbath school of about sixty pupils.

1816. In July a school was formed, also by females, in the Second Baptist Church, consisting of about fifty scholars.

1816. In August the females of the First Baptist Church followed the example, and collected a school of about thirty-five pupils.

1816. A Sabbath school, consisting of very young children, was formed in Northampton in 1816.

1816. In August, 1816, a Sabbath school was opened by ladies in New London, Conn., for children of both sexes.

1816. The Sabbath school in Framingham was established in September, 1816, by Abagail Bent, Martha Trowbridge, Mary Brown and Mrs. Charles Fiske.

1816. A Sabbath school society was formed, and a school established by the Rev. Dr. Morse and members of the First Church in Charlestown in October, 1816. Samuel F. B. Morse was the first Superintendent; and himself, Sidney E. Morse, and John Todd, were among the first teachers.

1816. A Sabbath school was established in Savannah, Ga., in 1816.

The city of New York claims, and is probably entitled to the honor of having formed the first society for the encouragement of Sabbath schools in this country; and this honor belongs to ladies. "The Female Union Society for the Promotion of Sabbath Schools," was organized by ladies of the several denominations in that city, convened by public notice, January 24,

1816. Schools for the instruction of females were immediately opened.

February 26, 1816, the gentlemen held a meeting, and instituted the "New York Sunday School Union." Schools for boys were immediately put in operation; and during the first year sixteen hundred pupils entered these schools.

Later in the same year, 1816, "The Boston Society for the Moral and Religious Instruction of the Poor" was organized, which early turned its attention to the establishment of Sabbath schools. The first school under its auspices was opened May 11, 1817, in the Mason Street school-house; and the second, June 15th, in the School Street school-house. Five hundred children were gathered into these schools the first season; and in a few years it had under its care in the city fourteen schools.

The era of Sabbath schools, as public institutions under the sanction of, and auxiliary to the church, in New England, dates its commencement with 1816. The previous efforts were individual, and preliminary; and though essential as a preparation, and test of means, and first attempts, were limited in influence. The plan was gradually getting together its elements; and fixing its rules; and awakening interest; and overcoming prejudices; and developing its capabilities.

How much the plan had to encounter, we of the present generation are scarcely able to understand.

The causes which delayed the establishment of Sabbath schools in New England, were, 1. The settled belief that family religious instruction on the Sabbath, was a plain duty, —made such, alike by parental responsibility, and the teaching of the Bible; and 2. A widespread conviction that the labor of teaching a Sabbath school was contrary to the spirit of the fourth commandment. This conviction was a natural sequence of the regard for the Sabbath *as holy time*, which prevailed at the opening of the century; and was strengthened by the well-known secular character of the English Sunday schools. The case is well put in the following extract from a letter of Sidney E. Morse, Esq.: "At that time, 1816, good people in Massachusetts regarded Sabbath schools as fitted only for the children of the poor, in such cities as London and New York, where the ignorant and vicious parents neglected the religious education of their offspring, and where no adequate provision was made for secular instruction during the week. In Massachusetts, where ample provision was made by law" (though not always by the local authorities) "for teaching every child to read and write on week-days, and where parents were presumed to devote a part of every Sabbath to the religious instruction of their children, Sabbath schools, it was thought, would be entirely out of place. Some of the best men that I saw at my father's* at that time, maintained that it would be actually a profanation of the Sabbath to open a school on the Lord's Day, as it would be doing work on that holy day which the fourth commandment requires to be done on the other days of the week."

The causes which led to their general opening in 1816–18, were: (1.) the good results which had attended the formation of classes by individuals and committees in many towns; (2.) the extensive revivals which visited the churches, and awakened Christian activity, and enlarged Christian thought in 1814–16; and (3.) the influence of one who came upon the stage of active life "for such a time as this."

The man who first comprehended this subject in its religious bearings, and to whom, more than any other, the merit of awakening and giving wise direction to Christian sentiment

---

* Rev. Jedediah Morse, D. D., of Charlestown.

in relation to the real importance and true relation of Sabbath schools, is the late Rev. Ward Stafford,* then city missionary in New York. It was through his influence that the New York societies were formed early in 1816; and it was a visit he made to Massachusetts in the summer of that year, which led to the formation of the Boston Society, before named. He enlisted such men as Rev. Dr. Morse, Deacon Josiah Salisbury, Sereno E. Dwight, William Jenks, John Todd—all then, or subsequently " men of renown "—in the Sabbath school enterprise, who at once began to operate on public sentiment. The Boston Society, of which the Rev. William Jenks was Secretary, prepared and sent forth a circular address to all the large towns in the State, in the spring of 1817. This address set forth the true object

---

* Sixty-two years ago Ward Stafford was a poor farmer's boy in New Hampshire. Becoming hopefully pious, he was placed at Phillips Academy in Andover, with only the expectation to become fitted for the duties of a country schoolmaster. A son of the Rev. Dr. Morse, of Charlestown, becoming acquainted with him, and appreciating his talents and Christian spirit, mentioned his case to his father, who at once solicited subscriptions in his behalf, and obtained of Deacon Josiah Salisbury and others, the sum of $700. With this money, young Stafford was educated at Yale College, where he graduated in 1812, with the second honor in his class, although among his competitors were such men as Hon. George Bliss, and Hon. John Davis.

and desirableness of Sabbath schools; and contained a well digested plan of organizing and conducting them. And it was this circular which led to the formation of Sabbath schools so generally throughout New England in 1818.

The Sabbath school was now a recognized institution; but it was yet in its infancy: what it would be, did not yet appear.

The number of schools organized in 1817, so far as is known, was not great; and the progress of the cause followed no regular law of outgrowth. Schools would spring up in different localities; usually the result of the efforts of some individual, whose heart was alive to benevolent Christian action, and whose means of information were superior to his or her neighbors.

In estimating this fact of the slow growth of the plan of Sabbath schools, it is to be remembered, that a half century ago, the means of circulating general intelligence were very limited. Up to 1816, *there was no weekly religious newspaper printed in this country.* "The Boston Recorder," the first of this class of papers, was started January, 1816; and the interest in such an enterprise was so small, and the desire for religious intelligence so limited, that at the end of the year the list of subscribers numbered only 1,300.

1817.

The list, already given, of Sabbath schools formed up to the close of 1816, is probably nearly complete. The list for 1817 will be less full; and the cases given are selected to show the similarity of movement by which all the early schools were gathered, and the common difficulties they all had to encounter.

"Braintree, April, 1817. Early in spring, the expediency of introducing a Sabbath school was suggested; but like other prudent folk we were afraid of new things, and had some serious qualms of conscience lest we should violate the fourth commandment, by doing on the Sabbath that which belongs exclusively to the other six days of the week. However, when we found that nothing would be taught but catechisms, the Word of God, and hymns, a few of us consented, and the school was opened the third Sabbath in April, with fifteen scholars, four teachers, and a Superintendent."

A Sabbath school in connection with the First Baptist Society in Framingham was opened, this year, by Abagail and Deborah Mellen, and Emily Parkhurst.

A school was gathered by young ladies, in Watertown, in the spring of this year.

"In Royalston, Mass., in the summer of 1817, a few young ladies endeavored to form a Catechetical Society on Mr. Wilbur's plan. It however soon became a Sabbath school, instructed by three young ladies, who had from twenty-five to thirty pupils, all females. Very little encouragement was afforded the school. In 1818, small schools were kept in four school districts, instructed by six females. In all the schools there were about sixty-five scholars. In 1819, a school was kept in the meeting-house, during the interval of public worship, under the direction of a Superintendent and twenty-five teachers. About one hundred and twenty-five children were constant in attendance, and fifty others were present more or less of the time. Besides this school, there were two others in districts remote from the centre, in which about fifty children received instruction from six teachers."

"A Sabbath school was instituted in Chatham (New Concord Society), New York, the second Sabbath in July, 1817, under circumstances peculiarly embarrassing. No efficient plan of instruction was then known. Many of the children lived at a distance from the place of meeting; most, of both parents and children, were ignorant of its nature and tendency; some entertained doubts of its propriety ; by some it was treated with ridicule ; while others exerted their influence to dissuade children from attending. Under all these forbidding circumstances, a school of one hundred and sixty different scholars was gathered, with an average attendance of ninety. One hour each Sabbath was devoted to instruction. Besides those who were taught to read, there were committed to memory and recited in sixteen Sabbaths, four thousand five hundred answers in the Assembly's Catechism, one thousand nine hundred Divine Songs and Hymns, and fourteen thousand six hundred and eighty verses of Scripture. The general effect of the school has been great. There has been an observance of the Sabbath by the children, hitherto unknown in this place." JACOB T. BENEDICT.

"On the 11th of May, 1817, three Sabbath schools were organized in Marietta, Ohio : one at Buell's school-room, under the superintendence of William Slocumb; one at the Muskingum Academy, under the care of Mr. E. Huntington; and one at Point Harmar, under the charge of Dr. John Cotton. To each of these schools several young ladies and gentlemen were attached as assistant teachers. In the three schools learners were admitted, consisting of children, male and female, adults, and people of color. The scholars have been employed in reading the Scriptures, committing portions to memory, and such other lessons as are usually taught in such institutions. Several commenced with the alphabet. The schools were continued twenty Sabbaths."

1818.

The great majority of the Sabbath schools in New England were formed in the year 1818.

In the spring of this year schools were opened at Natick (the second Sabbath in April,) Dover, West Needham, Medway, Medfield, Sherborn, Holliston, Dunstable, Groton (three schools,) Marblehead (a Sabbath School Union formed,) Lynn, Reading, Topsfield, Manchester, Athol, Warwick, Northfield, Roxbury, (Rev. Mr. Bradford's parish,) Northwood, N. H., St. Johnsbury, Vt., (three schools,) Gloucester, (first Sabbath in May, with twenty-nine teachers and three hundred and thirty scholars average,) Hamilton, (May,) North Bridgewater, (May, with one hundred and eighty-three pupils,) Warner, N. H., (May,) Thetford, Vt., (the church voted to establish Sabbath schools in ten different school districts, which commenced May 17,) Newton Lower Falls, (May 18, with eight teachers and sixty-four scholars, all very small children ;)—in *June*, at Farmington, Conn. (first Sabbath,) South Danvers, Woburn, Pittsfield, Vt., Stockbridge, Vt., (two schools,) Bridgewater, Vt., (two schools,) Hancock, Vt., (in the last named four towns the schools were organized by Rev. Justin Parsons;)—in *July*, at Conway, (July 12, with two hundred scholars and a large *Bible class*,) Bedford, (with eighty-seven scholars, from six to eighteen, under a superintendent and eight teachers;)—in *August*, at Dover, N. H., (August 16, with one hundred and ten pupils,) Danvers; —at Danville, Vt., September 20.

As sufficient facts have been presented to show that the Sabbath school had now taken a well defined position among the religious agencies of the Church, this list—necessarily incomplete—is here closed.

For several years, the recognized head, and authority, in matters pertaining to Sabbath schools, were the three Societies—The New York Sunday School Union, The Philadelphia Sunday and Adult School Union, and The Boston Society for the Instruction of the Poor—each operating in its own local sphere.

In 1824, The American Sunday School Union was formed; intended to embrace all the Unions then existing among evangelical denominations. In 1825, The Massachusetts Sabbath School Union—auxiliary to the Amercan Sunday School Union—was formed.

To these societies, and their natural outgrowths, the country is indebted to its Sabbath school libraries, and question books, and Journals, and books of song, and other vitalizing agencies;—till the " little one has become a thousand;" and the church cannot say to the Sabbath school, " I have no need of thee," nor the Sabbath school to the church, " I have no need of you."

[COPYRIGHT SECURED.]

TABLE OF CONTENTS.

	Page.
Preface,	3
Saturday Afternoon Classes,	5
Formation of Sabbath School,	7
Second year,	17
Third year,	24
Fourth year,	30
Fifth year,	33
Sixth and seventh years,	35
Eighth to fifteenth years,	38
Review of fourteen years,	41
Fifteenth year,	47
Sixteeenth year,	48
Sabbath School Society, 1818–1868,	49
Adult Department,	54
Infant Department,	57
Sabbath School Concert,	60
Benevolent Contributions,	64
The Library,	69
General Statistics,	71
List of Superintendents,	72
The School as it is,	73
Memoirs : Abner Stone,	82
Abagail Bent,	89
Luther Haven,	99
Mary Brown,	108
The Rise of Sabbath Schools,	131
In England,	131
Scotland,	136
America:—Philadelphia,	137
Paterson, N. J.,	137
Pawtucket, R. I ,	137
In New England:—Bath, N. H.,	138
Concord, Mass.,	139

TABLE OF CONTENTS.

	Page.
Beverly, Mass.,	139
Boston,	140
Brunswick, Me.,	140
Salem,	141
Salem, Tabernacle Church,	141
Newburyport,	141
Kennebunkport, Me.,	142
New York City,	142
Wilmington, Del.,	142
Cambridgeport,	142
Boston, Salem Street Church,	142
Northern Liberties, Philadelphia,	142
Newark, N. J.,	143
Chillicothe, Ohio,	143
Westborough,	143
Cambridge,	144
Providence, R. I.,	144
Greensborough, Vt.,	144
Carlisle, Penn.,	144
Boston, 3d Baptist Church,	144
Boston, 2d Baptist Church,	144
Boston, 1st Baptist Church,	144
Northampton,	145
New London, Ct.,	145
Framingham,	145
Charlestown, 1st Church,	145
Savannah, Ga.,	145
Sabbath School Union, N. Y.,	145
Boston Society for Instruction of Poor,	146
Era of Sabbath Schools,	146
Rev. Ward Stafford,	149
Braintree,	151
Framingham, 1st Baptist Society,	151
Watertown,	151
Royalston, Mass.,	152
Chatham, N. Y.,	152
Marietta, Ohio,	153
List of Sabbath schools formed in 1818,	154

www.ingramcontent.com/pod-product-compliance
Lightning Source LLC
Chambersburg PA
CBHW030435190426
43202CB00036B/927